Ethical Issues in Psychology

How do we know right from wrong, good from bad, help from hindrance, and how can we judge the behavior of others?

Ethics are the rules and guidelines that we use to make such judgements. Often there are no clear answers, which makes this subject both interesting and potentially frustrating. In this book the authors offer readers the opportunity to develop and express their own opinions in relation to ethics in psychology.

There are many psychological studies that appear to have been harmful or cruel to the people or animals that took part in them. For example, memory researchers carried out studies on a man who had no memory for over 40 years, but because he had no memory he was never able to agree to the studies. Is this a reasonable thing to do to someone? Comparative psychologist Harry Harlow found that he could create severe and lasting distress in monkeys by keeping them in social isolation. Is this a reasonable thing to do even if we find out useful things about human distress? If you were able to use psychological techniques to break someone down so that they revealed information that was useful to your government, would you do it? If so, why? If not, why not? These ethical issues are not easy to resolve and the debates continue as we encounter new dilemmas.

This book uses examples from psychological research to look at:

- key ethical issues
- ethical guidelines of psychologists
- socially sensitive research
- ethics in applied psychology
- the use of animals in research.

This book is essential reading for undergradu
undergraduate students of psychology and related
as philosophy and social policy.

Philip Banyard is a Reader in Psychology at Notting
University. He has a long-standing interest in the teaching o
ogy at all levels. He was Chief Examiner for GCSE Psycho
then A Level Psychology with OCR for nearly 20 years.

Cara Flanagan is a freelance academic author and lecturer. She ha
published a wide range of books covering general topics in psychology
as well as research methods and ethics. She organizes and speaks at
conferences for psychology students and trains psychology teachers.

Ethical Issues in Psychology

Philip Banyard and Cara Flanagan

LONDON AND NEW YORK

First published 2011
by Routledge
2 Park Square, Milton Park, Abingdon, Oxon, OX14 4RN

Simultaneously published in the USA and Canada
by Routledge
711 Third Avenue, New York, NY 10017

Routledge is an imprint of the Taylor & Francis Group, an informa business

© 2011 Psychology Press

British Library Cataloguing in Publication Data
A catalogue record for this book is available from the British Library

Library of Congress Cataloging-in-Publication Data
Banyard, Philip, 1953–
   Ethical issues in psychology / Philip Banyard & Cara Flanagan.
      p. cm.
   Includes bibliographical references and index.
   ISBN 978-0-415-42987-0 (hbk) — ISBN 978-0-415-42988-7 (soft cover)
   1. Psychology—Moral and ethical aspects. I. Flanagan, Cara, 1951–II. Title.
   BF76.4.B365 2011
   174′.915—dc22   2011004751

ISBN: 978-0-415-42987-0 (hbk)
ISBN: 978-0-415-42988-7 (pbk)
ISBN: 978-0-203-18098-3 (ebk)

Typeset in Arial MT and Frutiger by Refi neCatch Limited, Bungay, Suffolk
Paperback cover design by Lisa Dynan

Contents

List of figures

Series preface

The **Foundations of Psychology** series provides pre-undergraduate and first-year undergraduates with appealing and useful books that will enable the student to expand their knowledge of key areas in psychology. The books go beyond the detail and discussion provided by general introductory books but will still be accessible and appropriate for this level.

This series bridges the gap between the all-encompassing general textbook and the currently available advanced topic-specific books which might be inaccessible to students who are studying such topics for the first time.

Series editors

Philip Banyard is a Reader in Psychology at Nottingham Trent University.

Cara Flanagan is a freelance academic author and lecturer.

Preface

This is a new edition of our previous book on ethical issues. We have generally updated and revised the text, including reference to the new ethical principles published by the British Psychological Society. We have also included a variety of real-life examples of ethical dilemmas to give readers a true sense of the conflicts that arise. These dilemmas illustrate the real problems faced when trying to conduct ethically sound research.

The authors would like to thank the team at Routledge (Lucy Kennedy, Rebekah Edmundson and Sharla Plant) for always being so patient with us and always being filled with boundless enthusiasm. Thank you girls.

Cara Flanagan would like to thank her partner and children for their willingness to remain friendly despite the fact that she spends more time with her computer. She also would like to thank her co-author Phil for his gift with words and ideas.

Phil Banyard would like to acknowledge the support he gets from his colleagues, family, friends and students in his work. In particular he would like to thank them for humoring his irrational rants against the world and everything. He would also like to thank the following for providing absurd and pointless behavior for him to rant at: media psychologists, weather forecasters, the management at Heathrow airport and Nottingham Forest football club. He would also like to acknowledge the support of his co-author Cara for her patience and tolerance. Maybe he will develop these qualities himself one day.

Philip Banyard

Rights and wrongs

1

What this chapter will teach you

- What we mean by ethics
- How we develop moral codes
- What we mean by human rights and where they come from
- The basic ideas behind professional codes of practice

In this chapter we will look at what we mean by ethics. We will consider an array of concepts such as morals, ethical issues, ethical guidelines, human rights, ethical relativism and utilitarianism, to name but a few. These can be easily confused by the reader (and by authors, to be fair) but we will try to work our way through as best we can in order to better understand how psychologists develop their ideas of right and wrong and how we end up with the ethical codes that guide our behavior.

How ethical judgements affect people

Anyone who works with people has to make judgements about how they should behave and consider what effect their behavior might have on the people they are working with. There are a lot of factors that might affect those judgements and sometimes people make decisions that later come to be questioned. The basis for these questions is usually a code of ethics. Look below at two examples of scientific studies that have raised some serious ethical concerns.

The MMR myth

In 1998 a UK medical journal, *The Lancet*, published a paper from a research team led by Dr. Andrew Wakefield from the Royal Free Hospital in London. The press conference that followed publication made claims of a link between the MMR vaccine (a three-in-one jab for measles, mumps and rubella) and a syndrome of bowel and brain damage in children. This report on 12 children triggered massive media attention and created the myth of a link between the MMR vaccine and autism. The impact of the report and the massive press coverage was to dramatically reduce the confidence of parents in the vaccine and to reduce the number of children who were given it. The number of children receiving the vaccine in the UK dropped from around 85% in 1997 to around 65% in 2003 (data from the UK Department of Health).

KEY TERMS

Ethics The rules and principles that distinguish between right and wrong, and guide our behavior.

Autism A socially disabling disorder that usually appears in early childhood and typically involves avoidance of social contact, abnormal language development, and 'stereotypic' or bizarre behaviors such as rocking.

The decision to immunize your baby is very important for parents who obviously do not want to do anything to harm their child. The problem with not immunizing your baby, however, is that it increases their risk of childhood diseases and this might have serious consequences. The press coverage put doubt into people's minds and a question mark appeared over the vaccine. But not everything was as it seemed.

To cut to the chase, the story ended in 2010 when Andrew Wakefield was found guilty of ethical misconduct by the UK General Medical Council (GMC). And how! (For a full review of the story you should go to the blog of Brian Deer, a *Sunday Times* journalist who unearthed a lot of the details; see Websites.) The GMC enquiry went on for 197 days and concluded that Wakefield was dishonest, unethical, irresponsible and callous. The original paper in *The Lancet* was found to be dishonestly reported and carried out on children without ethical approval.

In brief, before the research was carried out, Wakefield had made an agreement with a solicitor who was looking for evidence to use against drug companies in legal challenges. Wakefield received over half a million pounds from legal aid funds to find that evidence. He had also developed his own alternative vaccines and stood to make a fortune if the MMR vaccine was replaced. The children in the study had been recruited from groups already campaigning against the MMR vaccine. The researched procedures had not been put through the hospital ethics committee and the children were subjected to a range of intrusive procedures. Finally, the scientific data did not match the reports that Wakefield made.

It would be difficult to find a more comprehensive moral and ethical breach than this. What is even more remarkable is that some newspapers carried on ignoring the true facts and continued to support the anti-MMR vaccine campaign. There are issues about media ethics here, but that discussion is for another book.

HM

An entirely different story and one that raises some different ethical issues concerns the case of Henry Molaison, who is usually referred to as HM. Molaison died in 2008 after a lifetime of being an unknowing subject of psychological studies. The case study appears in most introductory psychology texts and concerns a man who lost the ability to remember information after a brain operation. HM is very famous in psychology and '… he has probably had more words written about him than any other case in neurological or psychological history' (Ogden & Corkin, 1991, p. 195).

HM (he was always given those initials in scientific reports to protect his identity, although that might seem ironic after you read about what the psychologists did to him) was born in 1926 and had a head injury at the age of 7 that started a lifetime of epileptic seizures. These seizures got worse over the years and in his mid-20s he was having uncontrolled grand mal attacks (health-threatening seizures). It was proposed to attempt a brain operation to cure the epilepsy and a surgeon called William Scoville performed a 'bilateral medial temporal lobe resection' (cutting out a part of HM's brain). On the positive side, HM survived the operation and his epilepsy became less damaging, but on the very negative side he had profound retrograde and anterograde amnesia. More precisely, he had lost much of his memory for the 10 years prior to the operation (retrograde amnesia), and even more damagingly he had lost the ability to store new information (anterograde amnesia). He had about a 90-second memory span, so he was effectively waking up every 90 seconds not knowing where he was or whom he was talking to.

The operation on HM was not the first time this procedure had been carried out and the results could have been reasonably expected. The surgeon had been pioneering this technique on psychiatric patients and knew the likely consequences. Why he carried it out is not clear but there are numerous other ethical issues here about the conduct of doctors and their monitoring by colleagues. For an interesting and readable account of this study you can do no better than to look at *Memory's Ghost* by Philip Hilts (1996).

The operation was clearly a disaster for HM, although he probably never understood that because he could never learn what happened to him, or if he did he would forget it within a couple of minutes. This was a tragedy for HM but an opportunity for any psychologists who became aware of the case. They queued up to study HM's memory, assessing it with all kinds of tests and checking out a wide range of hypotheses concerning the theoretical distinctions between long-term and short-term memory, and between **explicit and implicit memory**. They used all sorts of stimuli, including electric shocks and white noise (for a review, see: Corkin, 1984; Parkin, 1996). One of 'the most striking characteristics is that he rarely complains about anything … is always agreeable and co-operative to the point that if … asked to sit in a particular place he will do so indefinitely' (Corkin, 1984, p. 251).

The tests continued for 40 years until HM was in his late 60s and his mental faculties were starting to show a general deterioration. One of the psychologists wrote of the major contribution this work had made to our understanding of memory and commented '… the fact that he has no conscious memory of this work does not in any way detract from the debt we owe him' (Ogden & Corkin, 1991, p. 195).

The story of HM is commonly presented without comment in psychology books but ask yourself this: How did HM give consent for the 40 years of constant research and experimentation? He did not know what was being done to him or even who was doing it. Is this ground-breaking science or cruel exploitation of a man whose life has been ruined by experimental brain surgery? His brain is now kept at the University of California, San Diego, USA and sliced up into sections. Who agreed to this?

Ethical issues

These two cases highlight some central **ethical issues**.

1 First of all is the issue of **informed consent**, which refers to the idea that any participant in an experiment should be informed about what the research entails and asked formally to consent to take part. This basic human right was first recognized by the Nuremburg trials. During the Second World War (1939–1945), Nazi doctors conducted various experiments on prisoners. For example, the doctors tested the prisoners' reactions to fatal diseases such as typhoid, and to extreme temperatures by immersing them in freezing water to see how long it would take for them to die. After the war a 10-point code (The Nuremburg Code; see Box 1.1) was produced and this has formed the basis for many contemporary ethical codes in both medical and behavioral research.

2 The second issue is the one of *costs versus benefits*. All researchers believe that their research offers potential benefits and they recognize that there are certain costs. The difficulty is in assessing the benefits and costs, and then deciding whether the research is justified. In the case of medical research it is easier to assess benefits but, as we will see, this is much harder in the behavioral sciences because the potential benefits to others are less easy to define. These issues are explored again in Chapter 2.

3 A third issue is the modern expectation that scientists treat all people with respect and take all reasonable steps to *protect their welfare*. If we see some people as less important than others, then it might seem OK to experiment on them so that the more important people can have some benefit. The war-time experimentation was carried out on people who were regarded as less worthy of respect. We have to acknowledge that even today we do not grant all people

---

BOX 1.1 The Nuremburg Code (1946)

1 The voluntary consent of the human subject is absolutely essential.
2 The experiment should yield fruitful results for the good of society that cannot be obtained by other means.
3 The experiment should be based on previous research so that the anticipated results can justify the research.
4 All unnecessary physical and mental suffering should be avoided.
5 No experiment should be conducted where there is reason to believe that death or disabling injury may be the result.
6 The degree of risk should also be less than the potential humanitarian importance of the research.
7 Adequate precautions should be in place to protect the subjects against any possible injury.
8 Experiments should only be conducted by qualified persons.
9 The human subject should always be at liberty to end the experiment.
10 The scientist in charge should be prepared to terminate any experiment if there is probable cause to believe that continuation is likely to result in injury or death.

[Adapted from Katz, 1972]

equal respect. For example, in the UK we are happy to buy branded sports clothing that is made in the developing world under working conditions that would not be tolerated in our own country. This can only be based on the underlying belief that the welfare of Indonesian children is not as important as British children.

What are ethics?

It all starts with **morals**, which are rules to guide our behavior. They are based on a number of socially agreed principles that are used to develop clear and logical guidelines to direct behavior. They also contain ideas about what is good and what is desirable in human behavior. Ethics are a moral framework that is applied to a narrow group of people such as doctors, or maybe a particular religion, or even psychologists.

KEY TERM

Morals Rules and right and wrong to guide our behavior based on socially agreed principles. Ethics are a moral framework that is applied to a narrow group of people such as doctors or psychologists.

There are a number of terms that we ought to consider in order to try to make sense of them. They do not have clear-cut definitions so the definitions we decide to use might be a little different from some other books.

We start with *morals*, which are 'concerned with or relating to human behavior, especially the distinction between good and bad or right and wrong behavior' (Source: The Collins English Dictionary © 2000 HarperCollins Publishers).

From morals we move on to *ethics*. This term has two meanings: one is 'a social, religious, or civil code of behavior considered correct, especially that of a particular group, profession, or individual' and the other is 'the philosophical study of the moral value of human conduct and of the rules and principles that ought to govern it; moral philosophy' (both definitions from The Collins English Dictionary © 2000 HarperCollins Publishers). If you took an ethics course at university you would probably be more concerned with the second definition, but for the basis of a psychology course we are mostly concerned with the first definition: the code of conduct that psychologists use to regulate their professional behavior.

When we look at ethics for psychologists we might start off by stating some *principles* that form the basis for our ethical judgements. From these principles we might develop some *guidelines* for behavior or maybe *a code of conduct*. When we try to use these ethical principles and guidelines we sometimes have to wrestle with *ethical issues* that arise because of conflict between one ethical issue and another.

The distinctions between all these terms are not clear cut – one person's issue might be another person's principle. The various organizations that develop codes of ethics use the terms in different ways: for example the American Psychological Association (2002b) refers to an 'Ethics Code' whereas the British Psychological Society (2009b) refers to 'Ethical principles for conducting research with human participants' and 'Guidelines for psychologists working with animals'.

The labels are not that important but the debate is. It is all about right and wrong, good and bad and the way that we choose to conduct our lives. What can be more important than that?

Consequences, actions, character and motives

The ethics of a behavior can be judged using four categories: *actions*, *consequences*, *character* and *motives* (Daeg de Mott, 2001). When we look at *consequences*, we judge whether a behavior is right or wrong by looking at the result of the behavior (see Figure 1.1). If it leads to a result that brings about an improvement for someone's life, we might think it is a good thing. When we look at the *actions*, however, we look at the act itself, and consider what the person is doing. The category of *character* is concerned with whether the person is a good (or virtuous) person who is generally ethical. When we look at *motives*, we are concerned with the intentions of the person carrying out the behavior, and we consider whether they were trying to do something good.

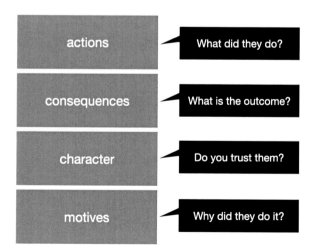

Figure 1.1 Judging right and wrong

Nothing is clear cut in the study of ethics and these categories sometimes give us different assessments. The puzzle is to decide whether *you* think the behavior is ethical or not.

REFLECTIVE EXERCISE 1.1

Look at the four criteria for making moral decisions shown in Figure 1.1, and then see how you can apply these to the following two examples. Do this before reading our view of this.

Example 1 Rapoff (1980) used an ammonia spray to punish a deaf–blind 5-year-old boy who was engaging in serious self-injurious behavior (self-mutilation), and in so doing reduced the amount of self-harmful behavior.

Example 2 Your government decides to go to war. The most controversial recent military engagement by the USA and UK's forces was the invasion of Iraq in 2003, and a debate is still raging about whether we should have gone in. Everyone (well, nearly everyone) is against war in principle, but the issue is whether in practice this war was necessary or right.

Reflective Exercise Example 1: Therapy

Rapoff (1980) used an ammonia spray to punish a deaf–blind 5-year-old boy who was engaging in serious self-injurious behavior (self-mutilation), and in so doing reduced the amount of this self-harmful behavior.

This sounds a shocking thing to do and many of you will immediately decide that this treatment is unethical but we are going to argue the opposite. The *consequence* of this action, if it is successful, is that the boy will have a better quality of life. The *act* does not look to be a good thing, but we might well judge the *motives* of the therapist to be sound because they want to help the child. Depending on what we believe about therapists in general or what we know about Rapoff in particular, we can make an assessment of *character* and decide whether we trust them to do the right thing. Considering that there are no easy solutions when dealing with very challenging children and that this solution at least avoids the use of medication, one might be inclined to judge this as an ethical treatment. Feel free to disagree.

Reflective Exercise Example 2: War

Your government decides to go to war. The most controversial recent military engagement by the USA and UK's forces was the invasion of Iraq in 2003, and a debate is still raging about whether we should have gone in. Everyone (well, nearly everyone) is against war in principle, but the issue is whether in practice this war was necessary or right.

The same four categories structure the debate. The *consequence* of the action is used as an ethical justification for the war. The removal of a murderous government is generally seen as a good thing, although history will be the final judge of this. The *act* of war itself is generally seen as bad because of the chaos, loss of life and general destruction that it brings. The bitterest part of the argument concerns character and motives. The US and UK governments argue that their *motive* for action was honorable and humanitarian, but some see their actions as being led by commercial interests such as the control of oil. The key issue for many in the UK is their assessment of Prime Minister Tony Blair's *character*. If you largely trusted him to do the right thing then you might have gone along, however reluctantly, with the decision to go to war with Iraq and continue to see it as morally justifiable.

REFLECTIVE EXERCISE 1.2

Think of your own example of something that has been publically debated as right or wrong, for example using capital punishment for people who kill other people.

- Is it ever morally right to kill another person?
- If you think it is, give some examples of killing that might be justified.
- Is it right to use the death penalty if one person kills another?
- If you think it is, give some examples of when it would be justified and also some when it would not. For example, what if a police officer kills someone in the line of duty, or an ambulance driver kills someone in a road accident, or a drunk driver kills someone in a road accident?

Use the four categories of consequences, actions, character and motives to decide on the ethics of these behaviors.

Absolute and relative morals

Broadly speaking, there are two approaches to solving moral dilemmas. Either you take the view that morals are *absolute* or that they are *relative*. The 'absolute' view is that some things are simply right or wrong. The absolutist position corresponds to common traditional views of morality, particularly of a religious kind – what might be called the 'Ten Commandments' idea of morality: for example, 'thou shalt not steal'.

Relativists, on the other hand, believe that all morals are dependent on context so, for example, they argue that there are situations where stealing is acceptable. The intrinsic 'wrongness' of an act may be overridden by other considerations: for example, it might be acceptable for a father to steal food because his children are starving.

As ever in these debates between two extreme positions, the common response is somewhere between the two. Most people who tend towards absolutism will allow for special circumstances and bend the rules on special occasions, while those who favor relativism are still likely to admit to some universal standards that form a 'bottom line' of behavior.

It is the generally held view in the UK that we should respect other people's property and not steal, but despite expressing morals near the *absolutist* end, many people behave in a *relativist* way. For example, most people will not go into a local media store and steal CDs, and the reason they may give for this is that they do not think it is right to steal. They might then go home, however, and log on to a peer-to-peer

---

BOX 1.2   Moral perspectives

Along the continuum of absolute–relative there are a number of moral perspectives. The deontological perspective (e.g. Immanuel Kant) holds that there are things that are intrinsically right or wrong but there may be exceptional circumstances that can override this position. It is largely an absolutist position. Deontological ethics emphasize universal imperatives such as moral laws, duties, obligations, prohibitions, and so on (sometimes this is also called 'imperativism').

Ethical relativism is the view that ethical judgements are true or false only relative to a particular context. So if I say that eating people is wrong, while you say it is right, we may both be speaking the truth. For cannibalism may be wrong in my context and right in yours. Morals are relative to historical or cultural contexts.

Utilitarianism (e.g. John Stuart Mill) says simply that an action is right or wrong depending upon its consequences, such as its effects on society (sometimes this is also called 'consequentialism'). An act is good or moral if it produces the greatest well-being for everyone affected by it. The cost–benefit approach taken by most ethical codes is based on this idea of consequences or utility.

site and download music to download onto their own ipods. This is theft just as much as swiping CDs from the media store. The reasons given for this theft might be that 'the record companies charge too much for music and are exploiting us', which would suggest high moral principles, or 'I won't get caught', which suggests that morals are determined by reward and punishment.

Another example is the act of telling lies. Most of us would say that we are truthful people who are not liars. But be honest, you give information to people every day that is not the truth, the whole truth and nothing but the truth. Some of these untruths are acts of politeness or support: for example, 'of course you don't look fat in that', or 'I'm sure nobody noticed you farting in the middle of the lecture'. Sometimes the untruths serve our own interests: for example, 'I'd love to come to your party but I've got to visit my nan'. We are not really liars, it is just that we do not tell the truth all the time.

It is very difficult to keep to an absolutist line, even though we try. As a result it is very easy to call someone a hypocrite because they appear to be doing something that they do not believe in. See Box 1.2 for more discussion of the relativist–absolutist debate.

> ### KEY TERMS
>
> **Deontological perspective** An approach to morality based on the idea of obligation or duty. Deontology is not necessarily an absolutist position because some deontologists believe it is morally acceptable to disobey a rule if the consequences are bad, such as refusing to tell the truth if it will harm someone.
>
> **Ethical relativism** The view that there are no objective, universal morals, they are all relative to time and place.
>
> **Utilitarianism** A theoretical framework for morality where decisions about what is right or wrong are based on the principle of what is useful or practical for the majority of people. Established by weighing costs and benefits for individuals and society.

Rights and values

Many people claim that there is a 'right to work' or a 'right to good health care' or a 'right to have children', but what are 'rights'? This is more controversial than you might think. It depends, in part, on where you think rights come from. According to Fukuyama (2001) there are three lines of argument about the source of rights: divine rights, natural rights or rights from custom and practice. In other words, rights can come from *God*, or from *nature* or from *human beings*.

In a religious society, the rights are seen to come from the God of that society, and are commonly written in a holy book and interpreted by religious scholars. If we do not believe in divine rights we might argue that rights come from the second source – nature – and that we should look at human nature to see what people are capable of and what can be viewed as right or wrong. The issue here is to describe human nature and to say what parts of our behavior are inevitable and what parts are created by the world we live in. This is clearly tricky because the world we live in has been created by ourselves and so we can end up in a circular argument – society affects the behavior of people but people affect the structure of society. It is also not a popular argument with liberals because the study of human nature can give us an uncomfortable picture of ourselves as selfish, murderous and xenophobic.

The third possible source of human rights is human beings themselves. The executive director of Amnesty International, William F. Schulz, argues that human rights should not be concerned with human nature but with the things 'human beings possess or can claim' (Schulz, 2000), or, in other words, human rights are anything we agree them to be. An example of this approach is the United Nations' Universal Declaration of Human Rights (1948; see Box 1.3 and Figure 1.2). This was a political document written to keep both the United States and the Soviet Union happy at a time when the Cold War conflict was just beginning. If you read through it you will find some absurdities such as Article 24, which states we have a right to 'periodic holidays with pay'. In a world where less than half of the population have paid employment, this is nonsense. And what about Article 19, the right to freedom of expression? This sounds fine and dandy, but

Figure 1.2 The Universal Declaration of Human Rights, hot off the press in 1948. © the UN.

BOX 1.3   An outline of the United Nations' Universal Declaration of Human Rights (1948)

Article 1. All human beings are born free and equal in dignity and rights.

Article 2. Everyone is entitled to all the rights and freedoms set forth in this Declaration, without distinction of any kind, such as race, colour, sex, language, religion, political or other opinion, national or social origin, property, birth or other status.

Article 3. Everyone has the right to life, liberty and security of person.

Article 4. No one shall be held in slavery or servitude

Article 5. No one shall be subjected to torture or to cruel, inhuman or degrading treatment.

Article 6. Everyone has the right to recognition everywhere as a person before the law.

Article 7. All are equal before the law.

Article 8. Everyone has the right to an effective remedy by the competent national tribunals for acts violating the fundamental rights granted him by the constitution or by law.

Article 9. No one shall be subjected to arbitrary arrest, detention or exile.

Article 10. Everyone is entitled in full equality to a fair and public hearing by an independent and impartial tribunal.

Article 11. Everyone charged with a penal offence has the right to be presumed innocent until proved guilty.

Article 12. No one shall be subjected to arbitrary interference with his privacy, family, home or correspondence, nor to attacks upon his honour and reputation.

Article 13. Everyone has the right to freedom of movement and residence within the borders of each state.

Article 14. Everyone has the right to seek and to enjoy in other countries asylum from persecution.

Article 15. Everyone has the right to a nationality.

Article 16. Men and women of full age have the right to marry and to found a family. Marriage shall be entered into only with the free and full consent of the intending spouses.

Article 17. Everyone has the right to own property alone as well as in association with others.

Article 18. Everyone has the right to freedom of thought, conscience and religion.

Article 19. Everyone has the right to freedom of opinion and expression.

Article 20. Everyone has the right to freedom of peaceful assembly and association.

Article 21. Everyone has the right to take part in the government of his country. The will of the people shall be the basis of the authority of government; this will shall be expressed in periodic and genuine elections.

Article 22. Everyone, as a member of society, has the right to social security.

Article 23. Everyone has the right to work.

Article 24. Everyone has the right to rest and leisure, including reasonable limitation of working hours and periodic holidays with pay.

Article 25. Everyone has the right to a standard of living adequate for the health and well-being of himself and of his family, and the right to security in the event of unemployment, sickness, disability, widowhood, old age or other lack of livelihood in circumstances beyond his control. Motherhood and childhood are entitled to special care and assistance.

Article 26. Everyone has the right to free education. Elementary education shall be compulsory.

Article 27. Everyone has the right freely to participate in the cultural life of the community, to enjoy the arts and to share in scientific advancement and its benefits.

Article 28. Everyone is entitled to a social and international order in which the rights and freedoms set forth in this Declaration can be fully realized.

Article 29. Everyone has duties to the community in which alone the free and full development of his personality is possible.

Article 30. Nothing in this Declaration may be interpreted as implying for any State, group or person any right to engage in any activity or to perform any act aimed at the destruction of any of the rights and freedoms set forth herein.

Extracted with permission of the UN.

in the UK we are (rightly, we believe) forbidden from freely expressing racist views. And if you say that the Holocaust did not happen then you can be sent to prison. In this case, rights are not absolute principles.

Since 1948 people have been enthusiastically adding rights to the list. It has become a wish list that has no end. Some of the new 'rights' highlight the difficulty of this process. If you consider the idea of 'animal rights', then you can see the problem. We would not want an animal to suffer unnecessarily, but does it have a right to that (a topic we will discuss in Chapter 5)? A lot of animal suffering will be caused by other animals. Lions chase zebras, cats chase birds, birds eat spiders, and so on. The issue is about human behavior towards animals rather than the rights of the animals.

What about our consumer behavior? Does a right to shop cut across the rights of other people? We might largely agree with the UN Universal Declaration of Human Rights but find we are compromising it by our choice of products. For example, if you choose to wear branded sports clothing it is likely that it was made in a developing world sweat shop where people are forced to work long hours without holidays and without reasonable pay. Their basic human rights (according to the UN charter, Articles 4, 5, 6, 8, 13, 20, 24, 25) are not being fulfilled.

In 1998 the UK signed up to the European Convention on Human Rights and we now have the Human Rights Act as part of the law of the land. If you want to know more about this then you can visit the website given at the end of this chapter.

Community or individual rights?

A further issue with the UN Universal Declaration of Human Rights is that it is largely about individual rights rather than community rights. So I might want to freely express hateful ideas, and as an individual it is my right to do so, but it cuts across the rights of the community to live in relative harmony and to be free from harassment.

The government of China locks up a large number of political dissidents but it can argue that, for Chinese society, individual rights are less important than collective and social rights. They might well favor the notion that 'the needs of the many outweigh the needs of the few' (Spock – closing speech in *Star Trek II: The Wrath of Khan*). It can be argued that human rights are largely a Western idea and we use them to claim the high moral ground while we continue trying to dominate the rest of the world.

What about the disputes related to the wearing of religious dress? The burka is a garment worn by some Muslim women that covers most of their body and face and means that other people cannot recognize them. Some European countries may restrict where this form of dress can be worn. The individual has a clear 'right' to be able to wear what they feel is appropriate and the community also has a 'right' to feel safe and to be able to identify other people.

It is a real problem and there are no easy answers here because negotiating and agreeing on how we should behave is a very difficult process. It is difficult enough agreeing who should do the washing up in the house, so coming to an agreement on how we should behave in society is almost impossible. The fact that we manage to largely agree on a code that allows the relative smooth running of our world is remarkable. The discussion about how we should behave towards each other is one that can never end, and each generation has to re-establish how it believes we should live. This means that the discussions about rights and morals and ethics must always be open. And this is what makes them 'issues' – there are conflicting values and we have no simple answers.

Developing morals and being moral

How do we develop our morals?

In the above examples we have considered whether something is right or wrong and we can see this as a moral debate. Morals are something that everyone has and uses to govern their everyday behavior. When we say that someone has no morals, we do not mean that they have no rules that govern their behavior but that they are using a different moral code from ourselves.

We start developing our sense of right and wrong from a very early age and over the course of our lives we structure our behavior by a moral code. Sometimes we break our own code but by and large people live by rules that make much of their behavior predictable and socially acceptable. This moral code is rarely written down or put up for discussion.

The term 'ethics', on the other hand, is commonly used to refer to a specific set of rules or guidelines that have been developed by a particular group of people, such as doctors, solicitors or psychologists. These rules are affected by the moral code of the society these people work in. Morals, and therefore ethical codes, are affected by culture and so change from one culture to another and from one period of time to another.

A number of psychologists have written about how we learn right from wrong and how we develop our personal moral code. Some might see it as a matter of learning which behavior gets rewarded and which gets punished. This is a **behaviorist** account of morals. Some psychologists make a **psychoanalytic** explanation and look at how the child internalizes the personality of their parents.

The most commonly described theories in introductory texts are the **cognitive developmental** accounts that emphasize how we think through problems to arrive at our judgement. The work of Kohlberg (1978), for example, looks at how children develop their ability to reason as they mature. He argues that as we mature we move from morals based on self-interest to morals based on principles. At the earliest level (pre-conventional) children defer to adults and obey rules to gain rewards or avoid punishments. At the next level (conventional) their behavior is guided by the opinions of other people and by the desire to conform. In the highest level (post-conventional) behavior is guided by abstract moral principles that go beyond the laws of society. Our choice of moral code will affect our personal response to an ethical code.

KEY TERM

Cognitive developmental An approach that focuses on how our behavior is influenced by the cognitive (mental) changes that take place as a person grows older, such as changes in memory, perceptual or intellectual abilities.

REFLECTIVE EXERCISE 1.3

How did you develop your sense of right and wrong? What do you think were the biggest influences on you? Who are the people and what are the events that have most affected your sense of right and wrong during the last year?

Legal requirements and professional standards

Ethical guidelines are not legal requirements. A person cannot be sent to prison if they infringe the ethical code of their professional group but they may be punished by their peers and/or debarred from practicing as a professional. One of the distinguishing features of any professional group is its commitment to be self-regulating and to police its ethical standards. Having said that, it has to be acknowledged that professional groups in the UK are very reluctant to act against any of their members. The General Medical Council (GMC) rarely strikes off a doctor even when gross misconduct has been established, and doctors who behave badly commonly receive only a censure. It can also be argued that psychologists commonly break their own code without being censured, but we will come on to that later. And as for teachers – they have chosen not to regulate their own profession at all.

Some aspects of ethical/moral behavior are policed by the law of the land. For example, the death of anyone is subject to legal scrutiny, so even the GMC had to remove British GP Harold Shipman from its register of practitioners after police established that he had murdered nearly 300 of his patients. You might argue that if the GMC had monitored his behavior and responded to his drug abuse and to the complaints made against him then the tragedy might not have happened (Ramsey, 2001).

The use of animals in research is controlled by legislation (e.g. The Animal Act of 1986) and the testing of drugs in research is also controlled. More recently legislation for stem cell research has been put in place. Any researcher who breaks these laws may be punished like any other criminal (e.g. fines, probation, custodial sentence), and their work stopped.

Principles, guidelines and issues

Many groups of people go beyond legal requirements to develop ethical principles (the moral values that are applied to their particular interests) and the guidelines or code of practice that is developed from these principles. Some sports people have an ethical code: for example, in golf it is unheard of for professional golfers to try to cheat. This is not the same for all sports: 'gamesmanship' or cheating (such as 'going to ground' or diving as some people might call it) is seen as fair game in professional football.

So the principles inform our guidelines and hence our behavior, but sometimes these principles create a conflict that leads to ethical issues. It is worth noting that there are very few right and wrong answers to ethical questions because we have to come to our own conclusions based on our own morals and our own interpretation of the ethical guidelines we are trying to follow.

Why study ethics?

It is one of the more difficult areas of psychology to study because there are no clear answers. That might well make it one of the more interesting areas for you, or one of the most frustrating. If there are no clear answers it means that you have the opportunity to develop and express your own opinion. As teachers of psychology we find it interesting to watch the development of ethical opinions in our students. Our own opinions have been changed by these debates. When one of the authors (PB) started teaching psychology some of the studies that were commonly used to illustrate psychological research involved cruel and distressing treatments on animals. I told my students about these without much thought. Over the years I found that students became more and more critical of these studies and after some (belated) thought I decided to drop most of them from my teaching and only use the remaining ones with very strong health warnings.

The study of ethics allows us to reflect on our own behavior and so change it for the better. It also allows us to reflect on the behavior of psychologists, to give a better understanding of the subject and, pragmatically, to give us some great evaluative points for essays.

In the rest of this book we will look further at ethical issues and ethical guidelines. Ethics are often used in a very narrow way in psychology to assess how we carry out our research but there are some wider ethical issues to consider alongside the practical guidelines. We will also consider the issues around using animals in psychological research. Finally we will consider the conduct of psychologists and the ways in which they continue to behave in ethically dubious ways.

Summary

In this chapter we have considered morals, rights and ethical issues. *Morals* are judgements of right and wrong in human behavior. It is not always easy to work out what is right and wrong, and this gives rise to moral issues. There are no absolutes in the area of moral behavior – but people have attempted to establish certain universal *rights*. *Ethics* are the morals of a professional group, and ethical guidelines or principles are established as a means of helping to resolve the ethical issues that arise. In ethics, as in morals, there are often dilemmas about what is clearly right or clearly wrong.

FURTHER READING

- Bershoff, D.N. (2008) *Ethical Conflicts in Psychology* (4th edition). Washington, DC: American Psychological Association. [A comprehensive textbook covering many different ethical issues and conflicts, presented by a range of authors.]
- Kimmel, A.J. (2007) *Ethical Issues in Behavioral Research*. Oxford: Blackwell. [Many of the issues raised in this chapter, and the rest of the book, are discussed in this book by Kimmel, which is a classic textbook on ethical issues.]

WEBSITES

- Ben Goldacre's take on the MMR myth:
  www.badscience.net/2008/08/the-medias-mmr-hoax/
- Brian Deer's review of the MMR story:
  http://briandeer.com/mmr/lancet-summary.htm
- Human Rights Act:
  http://news.bbc.co.uk/hi/english/static/in_depth/uk/2000/human_
  rights/default.stm
- New York Times obituary for HM :
  www.nytimes.com/2008/12/05/us/05hm.html?r=1&pagewanted=1&em
- United Nations' Universal Declaration of Human Rights:
  http://www.un.org/en/documents/udhr/

Ethical issues and how to deal with them

2

What this chapter will teach you

- The ethical issues that arise in research
- How these differ from the point of view of the participant, profession, researcher and society
- How we can justify doing unethical research
- Strategies used to deal with ethical issues

In this chapter we will look at ethical issues, that is, the dilemmas that arise when designing psychological research and the moral principles we use to assess whether our psychological research is good or bad, right or wrong. First we will look at some general ethical principles and the issues that arise from them. We will then look at how breaking ethical guidelines can sometimes be justified. Finally we will look at whether we can resolve any of these issues. You will note that nothing is black and white, which may frustrate some of you while being quite intriguing for others.

Ethical principles and the issues they bring up

I observed a mature and initially poised businessman enter the laboratory smiling and confident. Within 20 minutes he was reduced to a twitching, stuttering wreck … he constantly pulled his earlobe, and twisted his hands. At one point he pushed his fist into his forehead and muttered: 'Oh my God, let's stop it'. Yet he continued to respond to every word of the experimenter.

(Milgram, 1963, p. 377)

It may seem beyond belief that this is a description of a participant in a psychology experiment (Milgram's classic study of obedience, outlined in Box 2.1). Why would anyone permit such suffering to continue? From the participant's point of view the issue is one of psychological harm. From society's point of view this harm may be balanced by the potential for increased knowledge that may save or improve lives. The issue is one of *relative* morality. The psychologist conducting the research may be torn between responsibilities towards both the individual and society.

Equally chilling and less well known are the instructions given by Zimbardo to the research participants who had been given the role of guard in his famous Stanford Prison Experiment (website details given at the end of this chapter). In this study, a group of ordinary young men were assigned to play the part of guard or prisoner in a pretend prison set up in the basement of the psychology department. This study is commonly believed to show how the uniform of a guard may transform ordinary, 'normal' individuals into abusive and dominating guards simply because they are conforming to a role. However, before you accept this interpretation, you should read Zimbardo's instructions to the guards:

> You can create in the prisoners feelings of boredom, a sense of fear to some degree, you can create a notion of arbitrariness

---

BOX 2.1 Milgram's obedience experiment

Stanley Milgram suggested that one explanation for the behavior of Germans during World War II was their obedient nature – they obeyed orders from above. In order to test whether some people are more obedient than others he devised an experimental set-up. Two people are recruited for a study and randomly assigned the role of learner or teacher. The study is ostensibly about the ability to learn word pairs. The true participant always ends up as the teacher and the learner is actually a confederate. A third participant (again a confederate) plays the role of experimenter. The teacher must give the learner an electric shock each time he makes a mistake. The shocks increase by 15 volts each time. At 300 volts the learner cries out in pain. If the teacher asks to stop, the experimenter gently insists that it is important that he continues; 65% of the participants (teachers) continued delivering shocks to the maximum possible level of 450 volts, beyond 'danger: severe shock'.

that their life is totally controlled by us, by the system, you, me and they'll have no privacy ... They have no freedom of action, they can do nothing, say nothing that we don't permit. We're going to take away their individuality in various ways. In

KEY TERM

Confederate An individual in a study who is not a real participant and has been instructed how to behave by the investigator/experimenter.

general what all this leads to is a sense of powerlessness. That is, in this situation we'll have all the power and they'll have none.

(Zimbardo, 1989, quoted in Haslam & Reicher, 2003, p. 3)

Zimbardo is clearly inciting the pretend guards to behave in abusive ways, and a close inspection of the above shows that he is putting himself in the role of leader of this abuse (Haslam & Reicher, 2003). Note that he says 'we're going to take away their individuality' and 'we'll have all the power, thereby including himself as one of the guards. We will come back to these two studies in the next chapter where we argue that the Milgram study was, in fact, largely ethical and the Zimbardo study was not.

This chapter is about ethical issues; such issues arise because there are things to debate about how psychologists should conduct their research and, indeed, whether they should conduct it at all. It is probably fair to say that both Milgram and Zimbardo carried out their famous studies in good faith. They had serious scientific objectives and they very seriously considered ethical issues before they started and after they had completed the studies. The fact that we are still discussing the ethics of these studies after more than 40 years shows how difficult it is to resolve these issues and come up with clear principles that can be applied to every situation.

The next section deals with some ethical principles and gives some examples of the issues and problems they pose for psychologists. Such issues can be considered from various viewpoints – that of the participant, of the profession, of the researcher and of society.

The participant's view

Respect, autonomy and deception

We would argue that: All individuals should be treated with respect and allowed to be in control of their own life (i.e. be autonomous).

Psychology experiments that involve deception are in danger of taking away a participant's right to autonomy and denying their right to respect. Consider Milgram's classic study of obedience. The purpose of the study was to see whether participants would be willing to administer harmful shocks to another human being if they were instructed to do so by someone in authority. Participants were told they were taking part in a study about methods of learning. In other words they were deceived about the purpose of the experiment. If they had been told the true nature of the study, their subsequent behavior would have been very different. However, they did know that they were taking part in a psychology study and they chose to take part and to continue with the study, so you might argue that the deception is not a major issue.

Harm

> We would argue that: Individuals should not suffer immediate or long-term harm, either psychological or physical.

In the case of medical experiments, such as the ones carried out to support myths about the MMR vaccine (see Chapter 1), the potential harm is physical. Another medical example concerns the use of psychiatric medicines, which can have long-term as well as short-term consequences.

In some psychology experiments participants may experience physical harm. Milgram (1963) reported that three participants experienced 'full-blown uncontrollable seizures'. But, for the most part the risk, in psychological experiments, is temporary or permanent *psychological* harm.

BOX 2.2 Genie

Genie was brought up in terrible conditions for the first 13 years of her life, during which she was continually restrained by her father – locked in a room and often strapped to a chair – and rarely spoken to. When she was discovered she looked like a child of 8 and was unable to speak. She seemed to be an ideal case to use for answering a number of scientific questions about the development of language. The courts decided that she should be placed in care and one of the psychologists documenting her recovery took her into his own home. However, when the research money ran out and the study ended she was placed with a variety of foster families, including one home where she was abused again (Rymer, 1993).

There are numerous examples of individuals who have special qualities or who have lived in unusual situations and have been studied by psychologists because of their importance for psychological theories. As a result they have sometimes become the victims of psychology. A classic example of psychological harm, cited on most lists of unethical studies, is that of a young woman known as Genie whose case is described in Box 2.2. It would seem that the psychologists' interest in her was largely scientific, to the detriment of her own emotional recovery. In fact Genie's mother later successfully sued some of the psychologists involved for 'extreme, unreasonable, and outrageously intensive testing, experimentation, and observation' (Rymer, 1993).

Some cases of harm in psychological research are not as dramatic or immediately obvious. Consider the **Strange Situation technique** developed by Mary Ainsworth in the 1960s as a method to assess how securely an infant is attached to his or her mother. This technique has been widely used and adapted in hundreds of studies on attachment. The basis of the technique is to place an infant in a mildly stressful situation in order to observe how the infant responds. The distress is created by the mother briefly leaving the infant in a room on its own and, later, in a room with a stranger. Most infants become quite upset. In cases of extreme distress the researchers stop the study, but what of the others who are just mildly distressed? The argument is that any distress equivalent to that experienced in everyday life is acceptable, but is it?

KEY TERM

Strange Situation technique Method to assess strength of attachment, conducted in a novel environment and involving eight episodes. An infant's behavior is observed as mother leaves and returns, and when with a stranger.

So far these seem like clear-cut cases of harm, ranging from major to minor, but sometimes harm may be much more subtle. Consider a study by Carol Dweck (1975) that has formed the basis of a powerful theory of intelligence – the extent to which you believe that intelligence is related to effort rather than ability has a profound effect on your motivation to learn. People can be classed as ability- or effort-oriented. In the study (Box 2.3) this orientation was manipulated so that some children were led to believe that their success was due to their ability (Group 2) whereas others were led to believe that ultimate success was related to effort (Group 1). This study may have changed the way the children subsequently approached their school work. From the point of view of research ethics, does this count as psychological harm?

> **BOX 2.3   Dweck's (1975) study of task performance**
>
> In this study shoolchildren were divided into two groups. Over a period of a month students in Group 1 were given feedback about their performance – they were persistently told that the reason they had not done well in their school work was because they were lazy and should try harder.
>
> Students in Group 2 were always given positive feedback, for example they were told 'this work is very good but you might just include a bit more evaluation'. In other words, they were always praised.
>
> At the end of the month the second group showed low task persistence – they were much more ready to give up when they did not do well – whereas Group 1 met poor performance by increasing their efforts.

You might notice that all of the studies involve children, which is a more vulnerable group where research manipulation is concerned. What about adults? One study that often appears in lists of unethical psychological studies is the facial expressions study (Landis, 1924) where participants were exposed to various experiences in order to record and compare their facial expressions. For example they were asked to put their hands in a bucket of frogs, look at pornographic photos and, finally, to behead a live rat. It sounds like *'I'm a celebrity …'* but is it harmful between consenting adults? By the way, the aim of Landis's study was to see if there was uniformity in the participants' facial expressions but this proved not to be the case.

Fortunately the history of psychological research contains few such studies but let us consider a more subtle example involving adults. Morris Braverman, a 39-year-old social worker, was one of the participants in Milgram's experiment who continued to give shocks until the maximum was reached. He claimed, when interviewed a year after the experiment, that he had learned something of personal importance as a result of being in the experiment. His wife said, with reference to his willingness to obey orders, 'You can call yourself an Eichman' (referring to the Nazi leader who claimed that his role in the Holocaust was because he was only obeying orders). Such comments must affect the way an individual feels about himself even if there has been some attempt at self-justification (Milgram, 1974).

You might argue that all of the studies in this section are 'old', having been designed and conducted before the more stringent ethical committees of today, but even today you can uncover some studies that will make you think twice in terms of potential harm. Take, for example, research in the Catt Lab at Sussex University (Field & Lawson, 2003). They have found that children can acquire a fear of certain animals just because they are told that the animal is threatening. Ask yourself 'how do they know this?'. The answer is because they tell children (as young as 6) that certain cuddly animals are nasty and then test this by asking the children to put their hand in a 'touch box'. The box is labeled with the name of the cuddly animals and the opening has a hessian flap so the children cannot see inside. There is no scary animal inside (it is just a cuddly toy) but you might imagine that some of the children feel quite scared. In fact they are scared, because that is how the researchers know that the initial verbal conditioning did have an effect.

To be fair, various protections are put in place. For example, a child who takes more than 15 seconds to approach the box is prevented from continuing, and all the children are thoroughly

REFLECTIVE EXERCISE 2.1

Read the information below, which was given to parents whose children were recruited for the study by the Catt Lab (http://www.cattlab.net/index.html). Do you think this is sufficient to inform the parents and protect their children from harm?

Briefing for families volunteering to take part in the Catt Lab research

Are there any risks of taking part?
All of the tasks that you and your child will be asked to do are safe and have been used with hundreds of children before. At most the tasks may create a short-lived feeling of apprehension but they will not cause any psychological or physical harm. In past experiments, using similar procedures, the children have enjoyed the experience. You and your child are free to withdraw from the study at any time without explanation and you and your child are automatically assigned a code so that your names will never be attached to the data collected, so the information is completely confidential.

Has the study been approved?
Yes ... this study has been reviewed and approved by the School of Life Sciences Research Ethics Committee.

Harm can come in many forms. We tend to think about harm as being something that causes either physical or psychological pain. But what about the harm that is caused by giving people false hope? It is understandable that scientists will be enthusiastic about their research and be keen to explain the benefits of their findings. Unfortunately, this means they sometimes overstate the findings and the benefits of their work. When these claims are about medical or psychological treatments then people might reasonably develop hope that there is a cure for their condition, and when it turns out that the effects of the treatment are not as good as first thought, how does that affect the patient when their hopes are dashed?

debriefed afterwards. However, 15 seconds of feeling scared is quite a long time!

The bottom line may be that it is difficult to conduct psychological research without some degree of harm, but what are we willing to accept?

Privacy

We would argue that: What you do and say should not be exposed to public scrutiny without your permission.

Westin (1967, p. 7) defines privacy as 'the claim of individuals, groups, or institutions to determine for themselves when, how and to what extent information about them is communicated to others'. An illustration of this issue can be seen in the 'Tearoom Trade' study by Laud Humphreys (1970). Humphreys sought to demonstrate that certain common prejudices about homosexuals were mistaken. To do this he pretended to be a 'watchqueen' in a 'tearoom'. A 'tearoom' is a public toilet where men meet for sex with other men. A 'watchqueen' is someone who is allowed to watch the sexual activity and, in exchange, acts as a lookout. When apparently watching out for danger Humphreys also made a note of the license plate numbers of the visitors to the tearoom. Later he was able to access the addresses of the car owners and he interviewed them at home, claiming to be a health services worker. After this he destroyed the record of any individuals' names.

The main finding of this study was that most of the men involved in the tearoom trade led the rest of their lives as heterosexuals, often living with their wives. This confirms the common finding (e.g. Kinsey et al., 1948) that the proportion of people who only have same-sex relationships is relatively small, but the proportion of people who sometimes have same-sex relationships is much larger. Humphreys might argue that he had protected the privacy of his participants by destroying the names but you can also argue that he

Nineteen eighty-four

Figure 2.1 Big Brother is watching you. You may think of the TV series when you hear the phrase 'Big Brother is watching you' but in fact this comes from George Orwell's (1949) book *Nineteen Eighty-Four* where everyone was under constant surveillance from 'Big Brother'.
© Random House

had invaded their right to privacy by observing them and by obtaining further information from them through the use of deception.

Privacy is a big issue at the start of the 21st century. In some ways we do not expect to have a great deal of privacy and, on the whole, we do not appear to be too bothered about it. Your cell phone is a tracking device so you can be located whenever it is on. The phone company keeps a record of your calls, both incoming and outgoing, which has been used to study friendship networks without the normal legal requirements needed for phone tapping (Richelson, 2008). For example, Eagle et al. (2009) compared cell phone records to data collected from questionnaires and showed that phone records provided a much more accurate way to study social networks than questionnaires, where people tend to be inaccurate about who they spend time with, what they do, etc. Such data, it is claimed, can be used to design urban environments or track the spread of diseases. It is also quite easy to listen in to people's cell phone conversations (Butler, 2009), offering great opportunities for psychological research.

REFLECTIVE EXERCISE 2.2

How would you respond to the following ethical discussion?

You are a member of a university-based Institutional Review Board that has received a complaint from a group of high school students about the ethics of research conducted by a psychology professor. In the research, the psychologist had sat in a booth in a restaurant frequented by high school students after school, and recorded how frequently the students praised or criticized their parents or teachers in their conversations. The researcher also recorded specific statements used by students when they were praising or criticizing. No names or identifying information were recorded. The students had learned about the research when a local newspaper summarized the results from a recently published article on the research. When presented with the complaint, the psychologist responded by saying that the research was a field study that involved public behavior, that no one was identified in the publication and that there was no attempt to influence or change the behavior of the students. When presented with the researcher's explanation, the students said they saw their conversations in the restaurant as private, not public, and that they thought the research was a gross violation of their privacy.

[From Canadian Psychological Association et al., 2001]

In public space you also do not have much privacy. Britain has the largest CCTV (closed circuit television) network in the world. There are at least 4.2 million cameras across the country, which is about 20% of the world's CCTV cameras (*Daily Mail*, 2009). In the course of a typical day, the average city-dweller can expect to be filmed at least 14 times. If they are very unlucky – or lucky, depending on your point of view – they may be filmed 300 times.

This CCTV footage records your behavior when you do not expect it and it can sometimes be shown for entertainment or profit. There are some attempts to restrict this. For example, a man whose attempted suicide was captured by his local council's CCTV cameras and released to newspapers and TV companies won his legal action at the European Court of Human Rights in 2003. The court ruled that Mr. X's right to respect for his private life had been violated by the broadcast of the CCTV footage. Mr. X said his life had been shattered since a film of him taken in Brentwood High Street, Essex, in August 1995 with a kitchen knife, about to slash his wrists, was shown to more than 9 million viewers in 1996 on BBC TV's *Crime Beat*. He was severely depressed after losing his job and learning that his partner, the mother of his daughter, had been diagnosed as terminally ill (*The Guardian*, 2003).

It is clear that privacy has to be respected by everyone, including psychologists, but it is not clear how much privacy people expect nor how much they will be allowed by our press, our surveillance techniques and also by each other. Oh, and just in case you think that what you do at home is private, then you might like to know that the Google search engine is able to keep a record of what you search on the internet (www.google-watch.org). They know where you live, and they know what you are doing there.

Confidentiality

We would argue that: Researchers must at all times respect a participant's right to confidentiality.

Privacy and **confidentiality** are closely related and in fact sometimes it is hard to distinguish between them. For example, if a doctor reveals the identity of a patient, is he breaking patient confidentiality or is he actually invading that person's privacy? If you invade a person's privacy (such as recording their telephone conversation), is this OK

KEY TERMS

Privacy A person's right to control the flow of information about themselves.

Confidentiality A participant's right to have personal information protected. The Data Protection Act makes this a legal right.

as long as the individual's identity is kept secret? Confidentiality is one way to protect privacy – if privacy is invaded, then confidentiality should be protected.

However, there are a number of situations where it is difficult to decide whether confidentiality should be protected (see Reflective Exercise 2.3), so perhaps it is better to think more carefully about privacy in the first place.

Subjects and participants

We would argue that: Research should be a collaborative process between researcher and participant, not an autocratic one of ruler and subject.

A further issue for participants is the balance of power in the research setting. Typically the researcher holds the power in the research setting because he/she knows what the study is about and knows the procedures to be followed. This often leaves the 'subject' powerless. This power relationship is reflected in the use of the term 'subject' for all research participants other than the researcher. The concept of a 'subject' may encourage researchers to be less sensitive to the needs and rights of individuals involved in research. In the 1990s there was a move to use the term 'participant' instead of 'subject' in order to reflect the much more active involvement of participants and to emphasize their important rights.

It is to be hoped that the change of the term from 'subject' to 'participant' is more than just a cosmetic one. It is not a good idea

---

REFLECTIVE EXERCISE 2.3

The following is a real example. If you had been the researcher, what would you have done?

A university researcher was conducting interviews to investigate suicidal cognitions in depressed individuals, and one interviewee made it clear that she soon intended to attempt suicide. The researcher felt obliged to report this to the appropriate authorities, going against the promise of confidentiality. The interviewee was then sectioned under the Mental Health Act to protect her from self-harm. When she was subsequently released, the interviewee sued the university for breach of contract.

[From Chris Burgess]

to re-write the old studies and start calling the subjects 'participants', because they were not. They were treated as passive respondents to the research situations set up by psychologists and they were rarely dealt with as collaborators.

This issue cuts very deep into the power relationship between the expert (in this case, psychologist) and the naïve (in this case, the general public). If we say that psychological research should improve human life, then we should include ordinary people in the process and inform them of what we are doing. Mind you, there is not a lot of money to be made out of that. It is much more profitable to invent something that people were doing fine without but now come to believe is essential, and then sell it to them. Our world is full of useless products that are testament to this process. Consider the role of the bereavement counselor. Up until the last 20 years or so, there was no such thing as a bereavement counselor, although human beings have been dealing with death for 2 million years relatively successfully. They have found ways to make sense of it and to comfort each other. Suddenly, this does not seem to be adequate and we need a qualification to discuss bereavement issues. You might argue that psychologists are attempting to hijack everyday skills and then sell them back to us. Part of the collaboration ethic requires psychologists not to exploit people for profit.

Researcher's view

We would argue that: Psychologists should endeavor to conduct research that is meaningful and will ultimately improve the lives of people.

The researcher must weigh the potential benefits of any research project against the costs to any individual participant. The difficulty is that science does not proceed on such a grand scale but instead consists of numerous research projects each of which contributes to the bigger picture. For example, in order to understand human aggression it is not possible to conduct one blockbuster study. Instead there have probably been millions of studies that each contribute a small piece to the jigsaw. It is therefore difficult to make a decision, on a case by case basis, about the ultimate value of a research study. This is made even more difficult because it is not until after a study has been conducted that we can truly judge its value. So maybe we just have to trust psychologists' good intentions and that their professional society will police any rogues.

The profession's view

We would argue that: Members of any professional group have a duty to protect the integrity of that group.

Imagine a make-believe country where it is known that most doctors are not to be trusted and often do not care whether their diagnosis is right or wrong. There are a few doctors who cling to their ethical principles and are very concerned to conduct themselves properly and with regard for their patients. However, they realize that few patients will believe them unless they get rid of the bad doctors themselves. People need to trust the *profession* as well as the *individual* doctor, so in the UK we have the General Medical Council (GMC) to ensure that all doctors behave correctly and adequately. To be fair, the GMC did strike Harold Shipman off the register after he was convicted of murdering hundreds of his patients, so nothing to worry about there!

Psychologists need to be concerned about the ethical treatment of participants in order to ensure that psychology continues to be seen in a good light, and so that individuals will continue to be willing to participate in psychology studies.

Psychologists (and other researchers) also need to be concerned about fraudulent behavior, which could bring the profession into disrepute (see Box 2.4). One of the best known examples of this is the work of Sir Cyril Burt (see Box 2.5). The remarkable points about this case are the very obvious flaws in the data and the many years that the data went unchallenged. It reflects badly on the process of scientific review, which is meant to ensure that only the best work is published.

Lack of honesty in reporting research may be more of a pervasive problem than many psychologists would care to admit. Methods sections are commonly incomplete (Banyard & Hunt, 2000) and omit details about who the research is conducted on, how they were selected and where the research was carried out. Result sections commonly report that a particular effect was significant – but what they fail to tell you is the *size* of the effect. If the size of the effect (e.g. the difference in average scores between Group A and Group B) is very small, then it does not matter if the data are significant because it probably does not tell us very much anyway (Clarke-Carter, 1997).

It would appear that 'crimes' such as lack of detail in reporting research and distortions in the conclusions go relatively unreported. If a psychologist decided to comment on the behavior and research of a colleague they might well be seen as a whistle-blower. The issue of

BOX 2.4   A real dilemma

As part of my postgraduate course we all took part in a project where we had to code children's behavior. Over the course of the study we experienced 'coder drift', that is, some of the students became unreliable. To investigate how widespread this was, my supervisor requested that all of the undergraduates in the lab complete the same four inter-coder reliabilities against my coding.

When analyzing the codings I found two students, Sally and Anne (made-up names), whose results were identical for two of the tasks. I knew that Anne had had the means to copy Sally's results, which were kept in Sally's pigeon hole. I put fake data in Sally's pigeon hole. Specifically, I flipped everything. So, if the child chose the left-side object, now Sally's sheet said the right-side object. Now, if Anne agreed again 100%, I could be quite certain that she had copied from Sally (because the alternative is that she would be coding the opposite of what the child really did).

Sadly, my suspicions were confirmed. Anne's final codings were 100% in agreement with the fake data: Anne was falsifying data.

[From Jessica Horst]

BOX 2.5   Sir Cyril Burt

Burt and his researchers reported data on the IQ of twins and used such data to argue that intelligence was largely inherited. Burt was a highly respected and influential psychologist and no one suspected that he might have invented the data until Kamin (1974), among others, pointed out a variety of inaccuracies and inconsistencies. It was also discovered that two of Burt's supposed collaborators apparently had never existed. By this time Burt was dead and therefore not able to defend himself; others have subsequently suggested that the accusations were exaggerated and some errors were simply due to carelessness (Joynson, 1989). See the website details at the end of the chapter if you wish to read more about this.

whistle-blowing (on your colleagues) goes against one of the strongest playground ethics – do not snitch. As a result, it is rare for doctors to be called to book (as in the case of Harold Shipman) and the major frauds or malpractice cases are more likely to be exposed by people outside the field of study rather than by their peers.

Society's view

We would argue that: The purpose of conducting any research is to establish knowledge that may be used to improve the world in which we live or to better understand ourselves and our behavior.

Research rarely sets out its aims as being to make the world a better place but, ultimately, that is the goal. From society's viewpoint the ethical issue is a utilitarian one – to balance costs against benefits. 'Society' places greater emphasis on the benefits, in contrast to individuals who pay greater attention to the costs. Even this apparently clear and worthy ambition has a difficult side to it. We might believe that the world would be a better place if there was, for example, more order, less crime, less waste and less anger. We might be able to achieve these through behavioral, medical or even surgical interventions, but in so doing we might well cut across individual rights in the pursuit of the greater good for the community. And that is what creates an ethical *issue* – trying to decide whose rights are uppermost or more compromised. Later on in this book we will look at socially sensitive research, which raises a similar dilemma.

So far we have looked at the ethical principles from the viewpoint of the participant, the profession, the researcher and the general public. We will now go on to look at how psychologists justify their decisions.

REFLECTIVE EXERCISE 2.4

A lot of psychological research is funded by governments. They have expectations about the results of that research. What happens if the research produces data that are damaging to the government? Look at the following dilemma and think about how you would respond to it.

You are a psychologist employed by the 'Grim Oop North Development Board', which is funded by the government. The government has asked the Development Board to conduct a needs assessment study of high-risk suicide situations and self-harming among young people. The government's regional administrator informs you that the government wishes the data collection to focus on the positive results of local initiatives and that there must be no publication of findings unless the government gives prior approval. You believe there is a conflict between promoting the well-being of the community and following the request of the funding source.

[Adapted from Canadian Psychological Association *et al.* 2001]

Justifying unethical research

Deception, invasion of privacy and harm to participants are all considered to be unethical, but are there situations in which such a lack of ethical behavior is acceptable? There are many ways of dealing with ethical issues – such as the use of code of practice/guidelines, a strategy that is examined in the next chapter. Psychologists also deal with ethical issues by justifying them.

Some forms of deception are not that bad

In many studies the deception that is used is actually very minor. For example, in many memory studies participants are not informed beforehand that they will be required to recall data. This is to prevent the participants from rehearsing the information. Most people would not find this objectionable.

In field studies it is almost inevitable that passive deception takes place as the participants are not aware of being a participant. It may be that the task undertaken by participants in a field study may be relatively harmless, as in the study by Bickman outlined in Box 2.6. In this case the deception is that the members of the public believe they are dealing with an embarrassing social confrontation from an unknown and unpredictable person. They might reasonably follow the instruction given by the research confederate, as it is the line of least resistance and the most adaptive thing to do. Is such an intervention harmless?

Christiansen (1988) reports that participants do not seem to object to deception as long as it is not extreme. You might, however, still challenge the Bickman study because it is hard to see what scientific purpose it serves or how it contributes to the common good.

If you were a participant in this field study how would you imagine you would feel? This means of assessing ethical issues in a study is called using **presumptive consent**. In other words, a researcher often cannot ask the actual participants to give their informed consent

---

BOX 2.6 Obedience on the streets of New York

Bickman (1974) investigated obedience by arranging for male confederates to dress as a milkman, a guard or in a sports jacket and tie. The experimenter then gave orders to 153 randomly selected pedestrians in Brooklyn, New York. The participants were asked to pick up some litter, to give the experimenter a dime for a parking meter or to stand on the other side of a bus stop. The study found that people were more likely to obey instructions from someone in a uniform and were most likely to obey the guard.

because this would spoil the study, but the researcher can ask a similar group of people and then *presume* that the actual participants would feel the same way.

Validity of research data

The reason why deception is sometimes used in research is that the research would simply not make sense if participants were not deceived, as in Bickman's or Milgram's obedience study. When conducting field studies, deception is often unavoidable. Is the answer that one should not conduct field studies? The main reason to conduct field studies instead of laboratory studies is to investigate more true-to-life behavior. In a laboratory, people do not behave in the same way as they would in the 'real world' for a variety of reasons – because a laboratory is a specially constructed environment and participants' behavior is governed by an unrealistic set of rules, or because participants know they are in a research study and respond to cues about how to behave (**demand characteristics**). We say that these studies lack **mundane realism** and may lack **ecological validity**. This means that field studies commonly have greater validity and the price we pay for this is deception.

> ### KEY TERMS
>
> **Presumptive consent** A method of dealing with lack of informed consent or deception by asking a group of people who are similar to the participants whether they would agree to take part in a study. If this group of people consent to the procedures in the proposed study, it is *presumed* that the real participants would agree as well.
>
> **Demand characteristics** A cue that makes participants aware of what the researcher expects to find or how participants are expected to behave.
>
> **Mundane realism** Refers to how a study mirrors the real world. The experimental environment is realistic to the degree to which experiences encountered in the experimental environment will occur in everyday life (the 'real world').
>
> **Ecological validity** The ability to generalize a research effect beyond the particular setting in which it is demonstrated, to other settings.

Costs and benefits

The main method of justifying unethical practices is with reference to the consequences of the research – utilitarianism. If we can see that a study has the potential to produce meaningful findings that can be used to enhance human lives, then we can balance this against possible costs. It can be argued that the Milgram study has given us an invaluable insight into the nature of evil and tyranny, and it is an insight that continues to shock even 50 years after the original study. We would argue that it is one of psychology's most important studies for that very reason. It is difficult to use the 'invaluable insight' defence very often in psychology because studies that are as challenging and informative as the Milgram study are as rare as a sunny day in Manchester.

Can we predict costs and benefits?

It is difficult, if not impossible, to predict both costs and benefits prior to conducting a study. Milgram asked a group of 110 students, psychiatrists and other adults to predict how participants would behave in his obedience study. The majority said that 150 volts would be the limit – a strong shock. The maximum predicted was 300 volts, which was just below 'extreme intensity shock'. In fact the majority (65%) of the participants actually gave the maximum shock of 450 volts. This shows how inaccurate prior estimates can be (see Box 2.7). It also shows why we need to conduct research – if you simply ask people how they think they would behave, they may not be able to accurately predict this.

BOX 2.7   Milgram's study – comments from a participant

One of the participants who obeyed to the end later claimed that his behavior made him confront his own compliant tendencies. He was a homosexual but had been unwilling to disclose this to friends and colleagues. His experience in Milgram's study led him to be horrified by his obedience in the study and this realization led him to re-evaluate his own life, where he realized it was morally weak to deny his sexuality. Thus participation in Milgram's study led this participant to become less obedient (Slater, 2004).

Can we measure costs and benefits?

It is difficult to quantify costs and benefits even after the study. How does one quantify costs and benefits? How much does personal distress cost? If the results of a study demonstrate that people are more likely to obey someone in uniform, then how much is that benefit? How do we cope with the fact that each participant experiences a different cost in the same experiment? For example, in Milgram's study some of the participants appeared to be relatively untroubled by the experience and some reported afterwards that they were glad to have participated because it taught them something important. Does this make the deception less 'costly'?

Who does the counting?

Costs and benefits add up differently depending on who is doing the counting. If we judge the costs and benefits from a participant's point of view, we might list distress and loss of time versus financial rewards and a feeling of having contributed to scientific research. The research itself has other costs and benefits, such as possible loss of self-respect for the researcher versus professional success. Finally, society might weigh up the potential distress of people in certain situations against the use of any knowledge to better human lives.

Who wins?

Cost–benefit analysis tends to ignore the rights of individuals in favor of practical considerations. The judgement about costs and benefits is made by the researcher or other professionals who sit on an **ethical committee**. A researcher may well overestimate the benefits of his/her work and underestimate any potential harm to participants.

Is the cost–benefit analysis useful?

Cynics might argue that the cost–benefit calculation raises as many ethical issues as it is meant to resolve. Diana Baumrind (1964) argued that the cost–benefit approach solves nothing because the intention is to develop a means of dealing with moral dilemmas but, in fact, one is left with another set of dilemmas. Baumrind also argued that the cost–benefit approach in a way legitimizes unethical practices. For example, it suggests that deception and harm *are* acceptable in many situations.

Justification of unethical research is not the only way to deal with ethical issues. We will now look at various other strategies that are used to deal with ethical issues.

Strategies used to deal with ethical issues

As we know, ethical issues arise because of the conflicting interests of researchers and participants. A number of formal strategies have been developed to avoid or reduce such conflicts and are outlined below (many of these will be discussed further in Chapter 3).

Ethical committees

Ethical committees are used in order to avoid bias when a researcher is left to make his/her own ethical judgements about a prospective research study. Most institutions (e.g. universities, research units) in which research is carried out now have their own ethical committee, which considers all research proposals from the perspective of the rights and dignity of the participants (see Box 2.8). The existence of such committees helps to correct the power imbalance between experimenter and participant. However, if all the members of an ethical committee are researchers in psychology, they may be disinclined to

Figure 2.2 An ineffective ethical committee

turn down proposals from professional colleagues. For this and other reasons, it is desirable for every ethical committee to include some non-psychologists and at least one non-expert member of the public.

A good example of how an ethical committee can deal with difficult issues is illustrated by work on partial replication of Zimbardo's prison study by Haslam and Reicher (2003). This televised prison simulation (described in Chapter 3, p. 68) wrestled with all the complex issues of harm, informed consent, etc. The report of the ethical committee can be found at the following website: http://www.stetay.com/experiment/fullreport.html

---

BOX 2.8   Are ethical committees always right?

The two following student projects were passed by the ethical committee at one university.

One study aimed to see if self-esteem and body satisfaction would be reduced by saturation advertising. The other study planned to ask passing students in the college refectory if they had ever been sexually abused but had not considered at all how it would refer students who were distressed by this.

[From Matt Jarvis]

Use of ethical guidelines and legislation

Professional groups develop ethical codes of conduct, which are a set of rules that can and should be followed by members of the professional group. These codes of conduct or guidelines are discussed in detail in the next chapter.

There are two particular items found in ethical guidelines that may help to resolve ethical objections: debriefing and the right to withdraw.

Debriefing

It is commonplace for participants to be debriefed after an experiment. This gives the researcher an opportunity to assess the effects of the research procedures and to offer some form of counselling if necessary. The researcher may also use this as an opportunity to find out more from the participant in relation to the research. For example, Milgram asked participants if they suspected the real purpose of the study.

Once the participant has been correctly informed about the aim of the study they may elect to withhold their data from the study; in a sense they are exercising their right to informed consent in retrospect.

KEY TERMS

Debriefing A post-research interview designed to inform the participant of the true nature of the study, and to restore them to the same state they were in at the start of the experiment. It may also be used to gain useful feedback about the procedures in the study. There are some who claim that debriefing is *not* an *ethical issue*, it is a means of dealing with ethical issues. However it could be argued that *lack* of debriefing is an ethical issue in the same way that it is only the lack of informed consent that is the ethical issue.

Prior general consent Prospective participants in a research study are asked if they would take part in certain kinds of research, including ones involving deception. If they say yes they have give their general consent to taking part in such research.

Right to withdraw

All participants should be advised at the start of a research study that they can withdraw from the study at any time. This means that if the participant does feel harmed or undermined in any way he or she can quit.

In practice it is not that simple. A participant may be being paid for participation and may feel that quitting is not a real option. Even if participants are not paid, they may feel awkward about asking to be excused. Many psychological studies use students as participants. Such students may not feel they can jeopardize their course standing by harming the ongoing study.

Ways to gain consent without asking

Some researchers seek presumptive general consent, as outlined earlier (see p. 38). Another method is **prior general consent**, as used in a study by Gamson *et al.* (1982). They tried to circumvent the problem of deception by arranging for participants to agree to be deceived. The researchers advertised for participants and when interested individuals telephoned they were asked whether they were willing to participate in any or all of the following kinds of research:

1 Research on brand recognition of commercial products.
2 Research on product safety.
3 Research in which you will be misled about the purpose until afterwards.
4 Research involving group standards.

Most people said yes to all four and then were told that only the last kind of research was in progress. However, they had agreed to the third kind and had thus consented to be deceived probably without really being aware of it. Were they still deceived?

The study itself involved the participants being asked to take part in a discussion that would be videotaped and used to undermine an employee's lawsuit against the large oil company that employed him. Some participants rebelled and refused to give permission for the videotape to be used. Afterwards, many of the participants reported feelings of anxiety and stress. One said 'I'm glad to have done it but I'm really shook up and my blood pressure will be high for hours'. Another called the experiment 'the most stressful experience I've had in the past year'. The researchers recognized their moral obligations and stopped the study before it was completed, but nevertheless participants had clearly been subjected to psychological distress.

Alternatives: Role-play

It is possible to fully inform the participants about the nature of the study and then ask them to *pretend* that they are actually participating in an experiment. This is what Zimbardo did in his prison study (see pp. 22–23) and there is good evidence that both prisoners and guards took their roles very seriously, apparently forgetting that it was only make-believe. The prisoners took to referring to each other by number even when they knew they were not being observed. The guards became overzealous in their roles, and some guards even volunteered to do extra hours without pay.

On the other hand, it has also been argued that even though the prisoners and guards took their roles seriously they were actually only behaving according to stereotypes about prisoner/guard behavior that they had learned from films (i.e. they were behaving according to social norms). If this was real life rather than role-play people would be more likely to derive their behavior from personal rather than social norms. This means that we have to be careful about the conclusions we draw from the research.

In general Kimmel (1996) concludes that role-playing has not offered a viable alternative to experimental research, although there have been some successes. For example, Greenberg (1967) repeated a study first conducted by Schachter (1959). In the original study some participants were told that they were going to receive painful electric shocks, while others had no reason to believe the experiment would be stressful. Schachter found that those expecting shocks were more likely to seek the company of others who they thought were also anxious, supporting the hypothesis that 'misery loves (miserable) company'. In the replication, participants were told the details of the experiment and asked to act as if it was real. The findings were similar but not significant. However, Kimmel reports that such successes have been limited.

Summary

The viewpoints of participants, researchers, the profession and society all differ and may often clash, leading to ethical issues. For example, participants should be treated with respect and their autonomy protected, but this may be difficult when researchers wish to pursue valuable research. Unethical research may be justified in terms of balancing costs versus benefits, and also by arguing that deception is not always 'bad'. There are other strategies for dealing with ethical issues, such as ethical committees and the use of role-play. Possibly the most important way is the use of ethical principles and guidelines, which are examined in the next chapter.

FURTHER READING

- Baumrind, D. (1964) Some thoughts on ethics of research: After reading Milgram's behavioral study of obedience. *American Psychologist, 19,* 421–423.
- Francis, R.D. (1999) *Ethics for Psychologists: A Handbook.* Leicester: BPS Books.

- Koocher, G.P. & Keith-Spiegel, P. (1998) *Ethics in Psychology* (2nd edition). New York: Oxford University Press. [Stuffed full of brief case studies to illustrate ethical issues.]

A number of research studies have been mentioned in this chapter. Read some of the original journal reports to get a feel for ethical issues. To obtain the original article give the full reference to your local library, who will obtain a photocopy for a small fee.

WEBSITES

- Adolf Eichman
  http://www.pbs.org/eichmann/
- Cyril Burt
  http://www.indiana.edu/~intell/burtaffair.shtml
- Genie
  www.feralchildren.com/en/showchild.php?ch=genie
- Milgram
  www.stanleymilgram.com/milgram.php
- SEORG The experiment (Haslam and Reicher)
  http://www.ex.ac.uk/Psychology/seorg/exp/
  http://news.bbc.co.uk/1/hi/entertainment/tv_and_radio/1779816.stm
- Zimbardo
  www.prisonexp.org/
  www.lucifereffect.org/

Ethical principles and guidelines

3

What this chapter will teach you

- The code of conduct developed by the British Psychological Society
- Limitations of using ethical principles to resolve complex issues
- To recognize some moral issues not covered in ethical principles and guidelines
- Milgram was a good guy

This chapter is about how psychology deals with ethical issues by trying to develop principles and guidelines for psychologists to follow. A lot of time is put into ethics and, on the surface at least, psychologists take ethics very seriously. The problem comes with the interpretation of the principles and the clash of interests that can occur. In this chapter we will look at these problems and try to unpick some of the complexities in the discussion. The first thing we must do is to examine a code of practice. We will then go on to consider what other principles could or should have been included, and what happens when psychologists break these principles.

What are ethical principles and guidelines?

Ethical principles are intended to be a guide for individuals on how to behave in situations that raise ethical issues. One of the minor problems to clear up is the use of terms such as guidelines and principles. We have already written about this in Chapter 1 and tried to suggest a distinction between all the terms. Unfortunately, as we pointed out, the different organizations use the terms in different ways. Try not to get too confused or worried about the distinctions between 'principles' and 'guidelines'; the important thing is the argument rather than the definitions.

The British Psychological Society Code of Ethics and Conduct

The British Psychological Society (BPS), like many psychological societies, has published a set of ethical principles with guidance on how psychologists should interpret these. The most recent revision of the principles was published by the BPS in 2009 and you can read them in full on their website (see end of chapter). The principles are not just designed for research psychologists but also for practicing psychologists (e.g. those involved in treating patients with mental disorders or those working in industry advising on how to improve the performance of the work force).

The BPS *Code of Ethics and Conduct* (British Psychological Society, 2009a) is a relatively brief document (about 30 pages) that explains how the code was developed as well as suggesting how ethical decisions should be taken. This extensive re-write of the code was carried out to deal with some areas of concern that had arisen over the last 20 years. These areas of concern are summarised in Box 3.1.

Along with the *Code of Ethics and Conduct* there are a number of other documents that give detailed advice on specific issues. For example, there are guidelines for psychologists working with animals (see Chapter 5). There are also guidelines for carrying out research with the National Health Service, and further guidance for carrying out research with people who do not have the capacity to consent to taking part. To respond to the explosion in research using the new technologies, there is guidance on the new ethical issues that arise when using the internet for research. There are also guidelines for good practice in the use of penile plethysmography, but we do not want to go there or even find out what it is.

The Code is based on four ethical principles: *respect, competence, responsibility and integrity*. Each of these principles is accompanied

---

BOX 3.1   The areas of ethical concern identified by the British Psychological Society (2009a)

- Multiple relationships – where the psychologist owes an allegiance to several different stakeholders.
- Personal relationships – where the psychologist infringes or violates the trust of a client or clients.
- Unclear or inadequate standards of practice – where the psychologist is unaware of, or disregards, the current systems in use by peers or others in similar work.
- Breaches of confidentiality – where rules and constraints were broken or not clarified in advance with stakeholders.
- Competence – where excessive or misleading claims are made or where inadequate safeguards and monitoring exist for new areas of work.
- Research issues, including falsifying data, failing to obtain consent, plagiarism or failing to acknowledge another's work or contribution.
- Health problems affecting performance or conduct.
- Bringing the profession or the Society into disrepute.

---

by details of the standards that are expected of UK psychologists. We will go through the ethical principles in turn and look at how they affect the behavior of psychologists.

Respect

We wrote about respect in the previous chapter. Everyone expects a little bit of respect but it means different things to different people: the UK government has a Respect Agenda, which is concerned with encouraging people to be nice to each other and behave as good citizens; the Football Association has a Respect Campaign, as it tries to get players, coaching staff and spectators to behave well towards referees; and there is even a political party called Respect. Maybe the term 'respect' has been devalued by its overuse, but in the context of the BPS Code it has a very clear meaning (see Box 3.2).

The principle of respect in real terms comprises several aspects, as detailed in the following pages.

BOX 3.2   Statements of values (British Psychological Society, 2009a)

1 Respect
   'Psychologists value the dignity and worth of all persons, with sensitivity to the dynamics of perceived authority or influence over clients, and with particular regard to people's rights including those of privacy and self-determination' (British Psychological Society, 2009a, p. 10).

2 Competence
   'Psychologists value the continuing development and maintenance of high standards of competence in their professional work, and the importance of preserving their ability to function optimally within the recognised limits of their knowledge, skill, training, education, and experience' (British Psychological Society, 2009a, p. 15).

3 Responsibility
   'Psychologists value their responsibilities to clients, to the general public, and to the profession and science of Psychology, including the avoidance of harm and the prevention of misuse or abuse of their contributions to society' (British Psychological Society, 2009a, p. 18).

4 Integrity
   'Psychologists value honesty, accuracy, clarity, and fairness in their interactions with all persons, and seek to promote integrity in all facets of their scientific and professional endeavours' (British Psychological Society, 2009a, p. 21).

General respect

Psychologists should respect people's individuality and not show any prejudice on the basis of age, gender, disability, ethnicity, religion, etc. They should also respect the knowledge and expertise of others. This is an important point for professional workers dealing with the public because there is a tendency to patronize the general public, patients or students. If you have not come across this, then fortunately you have not had many dealings with the UK health services lately.

Privacy and confidentiality

It is important to keep records of what you do as a psychologist but these records need to be secure so that personal information cannot be disclosed to anyone else. Any disclosure needs to be agreed with the person who gave the information or data. This sounds very clear cut but there are some puzzles around this issue, as you have to consider what you would do if someone disclosed a crime to you or suicidal thoughts. Should you tell someone? And what if you scan a person's brain and notice some abnormalities. You are not a doctor, so should you tell the person that there is someone unusual about their brain?

Informed consent

In any work with people, either as a professional psychologist or as a researcher, it is important that the clients are aware of the procedures they are letting themselves in for so that they can make an informed choice to proceed. This is especially true when dealing with children and vulnerable adults but is not always possible (e.g. when conducting research with young children), so judgements have to be made about who can make that decision. Informed consent means that clients should not be deceived about what is going on. There are some exceptions to this but the reasons for deception must be clearly stated and justified.

Self-determination

It is important that the client stays in control of the situation they are in, which means they need to be reassured that they can withdraw whenever they like and that withdrawal will not have any penalties or embarrassments. They are also free to withdraw their data from the research study if they want to do so.

Competence

There is more to ethics than just rights and wrongs; there are also issues about how well you do your work.

Awareness of professional ethics

Ethics are an important part of professional life and it is expected that psychologists make themselves aware of ethical principles and codes. Ignorance is not an excuse for making ethical mistakes, and in fact is a mistake in itself.

BOX 3.3 A question of competence

I (MJ) was in a taxi once and the driver was listening to a phone-in in which a psychiatrist was saying that psychopaths are entirely untreatable. The driver asked what I thought of that and I replied that this was actually a matter of some debate, with some clinical psychologists suggesting that antisocial personality disorder is indeed treatable, at least in some cases. Having asked me what I did for a living the driver promptly called his son who was presenting the programme and said 'I've got a psychologist in the cab who says your psychiatrist is talking crap!' The psychiatrist was not amused and asked who I was. Fortunately we arrived at my destination at that point and I ran away! The issues here are of competence. I saw the situation as simply chatting and offering an appropriately neutral answer to a question, as well as spreading psychological understanding, which is part of my brief as a teacher/lecturer. However, the situation could quickly have changed to one of me publicly challenging a much more eminent specialist, distorting the public perception of an issue and bringing psychology into disrepute.

[From Matt Jarvis]

Decision-making

Making ethical decisions is more difficult than it seems and it is important to be careful and thoughtful when making those decisions. This involves taking responsibility for any decisions that are made, consulting ethical codes and getting colleagues to look over your decisions and to comment on them.

Recognizing limits of competence

It is important to recognize what you know and also what you do not know. There is a danger in professional life to go beyond what you know and imply that you have more knowledge than you really do. For example, a research psychologist might come across some information during a research project that suggests the participant would benefit from professional help. In these circumstances the researcher should tell the participant and suggest some possible sources of help (see Box 3.3). It is not appropriate, however, for the researcher to start giving advice outside their area of expertise; if, for example, during an interview a participant becomes emotional and brings up distressing material, then it is unlikely that the researcher (not being a trained counselor) would be able to deal effectively with this.

The problem is that if a friend of yours is upset and wants to talk to you, then it does not matter that you are not a counselor – you talk to them as a friend. If, however, you have been introduced to someone as a psychologist, then they might well have unrealistic expectations about your knowledge and skill to deal with emotional problems.

Recognizing impairment

To carry out a professional job it is necessary to be in a fit state to do it. Sometimes we are not in a fit state because of our lifestyle, our general health or our mental health. It is important to be able to reflect on your own competence and make the decision to seek help and stop working. This is a tough call to make.

Responsibility

Psychologists have responsibilities to clients, the general public and to their profession. The last thing you want is to hear someone saying: 'You've let your clients, down, you've let your profession down, but most of all you've let yourself down.'

General responsibility

It is important to ensure that clients are not harmed by a psychologist's action or even inaction. This can create some problems because sometimes, by protecting one person from harm, you might put another person at greater risk of harm. For example, most psychiatric medication has harmful side-effects and some of these are permanent. The medications that are commonly used to reduce the symptoms of psychosis can bring on the symptoms of Parkinson's disease or the distressing condition of tardive diskinesia (where the patient develops permanent embarrassing facial movements). To protect the patient from harm you might recommend that they do not take the medication but this might result in an increase in their symptoms and put other people at risk from their disturbed behavior.

Other things to consider are ensuring that the profession is not brought into disrepute and also monitoring the actions of colleagues to ensure that they are also behaving ethically.

Continuity of care

Some therapies could go on for ever because it is impossible to completely sort out a person's life. Therapies can have an impact on helping people to improve their situation, behavior or mood but there is a limit to the benefit that can be achieved. The psychologist needs to recognize and respond to the situation where the benefits are no longer very substantial and suggest that the treatment ends or is conducted in an alternative way.

Protection of research participants

It stands to reason that research should not harm people and that all potential risks to well-being and dignity are removed. Harm can arise in a number of ways and not all of them can be anticipated (see, for example, the discussion on p. 65).

Researchers are asked to be aware of participants' personal circumstances because in some cases this might increase the risks for them in the research. The risks might be physical, such as a heart condition, or emotional, such as a recent bereavement. Also, researchers are asked to exercise caution when discussing the results of studies, especially with parents, because people sometimes put a lot of weight on the words of psychologists. For example, if you took part in a test on personality and the test gave you a high score on the *'Useless Loser Scale'* (made up name, I hope), you might be a bit distressed and take some negative feelings away from the study even if you knew that psychometric measures are not always reliable or valid.

There is also an issue about offering incentives such as money or course credits for students to take part in research studies. Many universities have schemes that give students credit for being a participant. Sometimes these schemes give tokens that can be used when the student wants to carry out their own research but with participants of their own. Sometimes they are used as part of the course and a student can only obtain a pass if they have clocked up enough hours as a participant. There is clearly a degree of coercion here and although it is possible to argue that the student is being encouraged to be a good citizen/student and help others in their research, it is also possible to argue that this sort of incentive is too coercive.

Debriefing

In studies where the participants are aware that they have taken part in an investigation, once the data have been collected the investigator should provide the participants with any necessary information to complete their understanding of the nature of the research. The investigator should discuss with the participants their experience of the research in order to monitor any unforeseen negative effects or misconceptions.

REFLECTIVE EXERCISE 3.1

As a social psychologist you have received a grant to study racial discrimination in housing. You plan to employ black, white and Asian students to pose as married couples in various combinations to enquire about apartments that have been advertised as vacant. You believe that the potential social benefit of the study outweighs any reservations you have about using the deception involved. However, you are not sure whether debriefing of the apartment advertisers is needed or wise under the circumstances. You believe that the apartment advertisers would not be subjected to stress or to loss of self-esteem by the study, and that they would have their self-knowledge enhanced when the results became public (without identifying the individuals involved). However, you are concerned that trust in the discipline of psychology might be undermined if no debriefing is done.

What do you think is the best thing to do?

[From Canadian Psychological Association *et al.*, 2001]

Integrity

Being honest and open about things is something that many of us aspire to but it is hard to achieve.

Honesty and accuracy

There are many people who misrepresent their training and expertise – the internet is awash with them, as are the sofas of daytime TV studios. It is important that psychologists do not succumb to this because it ends up devaluing the whole profession.

Research findings are often misrepresented and sexed-up to make them media friendly. Even though it is a dull thing to do, psychologists need to present their evidence honestly and not overstate it for dramatic effect. And on the subject of research, psychologists should not claim other people's work as their own.

Avoiding exploitation and conflicts of interest

One of the most problematic conflicts of interest concerns the overlap of professional and personal lives. Relationships with colleagues who are in a different position in the hierarchy of the organization are problematic, and relationships with personal students or clients are even more so. The central issue is one of power – and the psychologist will have more power than the other person in the relationship. It is obviously good practice to keep personal and professional lives separate but that is not always possible and at these times the psychologist needs to seek ethical support and approval.

Maintaining personal boundaries

The BPS Code is very strong in stating that psychologists should:

> refrain from engaging in any form of sexual or romantic relationship with persons to whom they are providing professional services, or to whom they owe a continuing duty of care, or with whom they have a relationship of trust. This might include a former patient, a student or trainee, or a junior staff member.
>
> (British Psychological Society, 2009a, p. 22)

Another aspect of the issue is to recognize the damage that harassment can do to individuals at work and aim to reduce this wherever possible. We will explore this issue a little further in Chapter 6.

Addressing ethical misconduct

If confronted about ethical behavior it is expected that psychologists will cooperate with any enquiry in a positive way. Also it is expected that, regardless of friendship or other constraints, psychologists will report any behavior of colleagues that they believe to be in conflict with the ethical code. This again is a tough one because it is one of the basic rules of human interaction not to snitch, but it is not acceptable to just turn a blind eye to situations you know are wrong.

Limitations of ethical principles as a way of resolving ethical issues

In the above section we have given a summary of the BPS *Code of Ethics and Conduct*. We will now go on to comment on them. This means, inevitably, that we will be interpreting the principles from our own perspective and showing our own concerns and biases. You might well have a different view.

Truly informed consent

The principle that gives the greatest puzzle surrounds the issue of consent. What do we mean by real consent and can we ever be fully informed about anything? The point about research, as Milgram noted, is that we do not know what is going to happen. If we did, there would be no point in the research. Therefore we cannot fully inform our participants. If we carry out simple studies devoid of any relevance to everyday life then it might be possible to identify all the necessary information to achieve real consent, but if we want to investigate how people conduct themselves in real situations we can never achieve this. If the consequence of this is that psychologists are doomed to carry out detailed studies of not very much, then their work will become 'impeccable trivia' (Reicher & Haslam, 2009, p. 469). Maybe we have to face the issue of consent head-on and recognize that we can never have fully informed consent. We will look at some examples of studies that have confronted this issue later in this chapter.

There is also the question of whether people actually listen to the information given to them prior to a study. When you have to sign a form that ends with 'I agree to abide by the rules above', do you actually read the rules? This is a particular problem with research conducted on the internet. It is the same problem we have with instructions for new equipment; we never read them until we have broken it.

Even if the information is conveyed to a prospective participant, they may not fully understand the implications. Knowing that you are about to answer questions that may be of a personal nature does not mean that you understands *how* personal these are or what the effects will be.

REFLECTIVE EXERCISE 3.2

The following is a real example:

> A psychology student wished to conduct a study on whether having breakfast in the morning improves memory. The research proposal showed that the student intended to approach people in her class as participants. Part of the procedure includes asking participants for a detailed food diary, which could be an issue if one of her classmates has an eating disorder.

The student had not thought carefully enough about what 'informed consent' means in practice. The participant would not be aware of a methodological detail that at first sight seems uncontroversial but to someone with an eating disorder could be very distressing.

Are there other issues that should be raised when seeking informed consent?

[From S. MacAndrew]

Deception

Psychologists always lie!

(Anonymous student quoted by Kimmel, 1996)

With regard to **deception**, it has to be said that most human interaction is based on a certain amount of deceit. We rarely disclose the truth, the whole truth and nothing but the truth. Imagine what you tell your parents and then your friends about your holiday in Kavos. Both stories are mainly true, but they are likely to be very different. You are not lying, just being selective. In everyday life we do not expect to be told the whole truth, nor do we commonly want it. When we ask someone 'How are you?', we certainly do not want to be told their current medical and psychiatric condition. 'Fine thanks,' is the answer we require. We expect to be told the necessary information, not the full works. This book is a case in point. We have not reproduced the full version of the BPS *Code of Ethics and Conduct* but have selected what we think are the parts you will find most useful in your studies. Are we deceiving you? Probably not, but we are not giving you full disclosure.

There is also the question of active versus passive deception. In some studies participants are actively deceived, that is, they are told a deliberate lie to lead them away from guessing the true purpose of the experiment (as in Milgram's experiment). In other studies passive deception takes place when a participant does not know they are being observed, or where researchers provide an incomplete explanation of their research project to participants because of the potential effects. For example, in one study researchers failed to fully inform participants that 'death anxiety' was the real focus of the study (Florian & Mikulincer, 1998). A subsequent replication that provided fully informed consent obtained different findings, which shows that gaining informed consent does have an effect (Tunnicliff, 1998).

We have to return to the **absolutist** and **relativist** moral debate we first looked at in Chapter 1. If we take an absolute line on consent and deception then most psychological research is unethical. If we take a relativist line, then we might say that most psychological research falls

> **KEY TERMS**
>
> **Deception** This occurs when a participant is not told the true aims of a study (e.g. what participation will involve), thus the participants cannot give truly informed consent. Deception may be active (e.g. the participant is given false information) or passive (e.g. information is withheld).
>
> **Absolutist morals** The view that some things are simply right or wrong, there is no relative position. For example, murder is wrong no matter what the circumstances are.
>
> **Relativist morals** The view that morals are not absolute but are dependent on context so, for example, in some situations stealing is acceptable. The intrinsic 'wrongness' of an act may be overridden by other considerations.

within the ethical principles. The difficulty with the absolutist approach is that you prohibit virtually all psychological research. The difficulty with the relativist approach, on the other hand, is that you still have to draw a bottom line somewhere because it cannot be used to allow *all* deception.

Confidentiality

The principle of confidentiality can pose some new ethical dilemmas of its own. What if you are carrying out some interviews and the participant, let us call her Cheryl, tells you that she has done a criminal act. Should you tell anyone, and break confidentiality? This would contravene your ethical principles, but not reporting a crime goes against the general moral code of society. Maybe you would judge it on the nature of the crime. If Cheryl tells you she nicked some sweets from the pick 'n mix when she was 8 then maybe that is OK. But what about if she tells you she burgled her elderly neighbor last week, or made a drunken assault on a nightclub toilet attendant, or maybe that she likes using a chain saw to cut up stray cats? It is not easy to make this decision. To disclose the information breaks your ethical principles, but to keep the confidence might lead to decimation of the local cat population.

Improving the quality of life

In Chapter 2 we suggested that:

> The purpose of conducting any research is to establish knowledge that may be used to improve the world in which we live or to better understand ourselves and our behavior.

This aim is echoed by some psychologists and, most famously, George Miller (1969) in his presidential address to the American Psychological Association (APA). Miller reminded us that the stated aim of the APA is to promote human welfare. He went on to consider what he meant by this phrase because it can be interpreted in different ways. One way to interpret it would be to argue for more control on our lives so that we are forced to behave better and hence improve our quality of life. If we had a Tab Patrol to check out smokers and force them to quit then you might argue that our quality of life would be improved. Many people might see Tab Patrol, however, as an invasion on personal liberty and start muttering phrases like 'health fascists' and 'nanny state'. Miller's argument was not to improve life by controlling people but to suggest that psychology can contribute to quality of life by encouraging a better understanding of ourselves so that we can be more aware of 'what is humanly possible and humanly desirable'.

In his view, we are all psychologists. Every day we make judgements about our own behavior and the behavior of others. Just to engage in a casual conversation with someone I have to make a mental model of what you are thinking and feeling and then match my words accordingly. Some psychology acknowledges this, but some psychology seeks to create an expert status for psychologists as people who know lots more about life and behavior than ordinary people can ever hope to know. Miller (1969) does not buy into this and suggests that 'Our responsibility is less to assume the role of experts and try to apply psychology ourselves than to give it away to the people who really need it' (p. 1065).

Whatever view you take on the 'psychologist as expert' issue, you might well think that it is important for psychological research to make a useful contribution either to our knowledge or to the application of the subject. You might well suggest that there should be an additional ethical principle of *usefulness*, and that psychological research is required to demonstrate that it is making a contribution to improve the world we live in.

Racism

Racism is a social dilemma for each generation to wrestle with. Psychology has an uncomfortable past with race science and has sometimes provided a platform for racially offensive views. We would not deny that there might be some psychological questions to ask about race but there are so many scientific and political objections to this approach. In the first place we can only investigate racial differences if we can first define what race is and then carry out appropriate studies. As Jones (1991) points out, there are a number of problems, including:

- the difficulty in defining race
- the history of social movement, which has meant that many people have ancestors from many parts of the world
- within-race variability is much greater than between-race variability
- when comparative research is carried out, it has so far been impossible to obtain comparable samples of people from different races.

On the specific issue of IQ, the UK's first professor of psychometrics, Paul Kline, wrote:

> ... The only advantage in setting out the different scores on IQ tests of racial groups is to give ammunition to those who wish to decry them. It adds nothing to theoretical understanding or to the social or educational practice.
>
> (Kline, 1991, p. 96)

This analysis makes the enduring debate about racial differences all the more remarkable. You might hope that serious scientific and professional journals are careful and measured in their approach to this topic, given its potential for mischief and harm. Unfortunately this is not always the case and even the BPS in its professional journal, *The Psychologist*, chose to publish an article by academic controversialist J. Philippe Rushton (1990) that put forward an academically shallow but openly racist set of ideas. The article used evidence that was scientifically flawed to put forward a case for racial superiority of some races over others. The poor level of the science should have been enough to reject the article, regardless of the unfounded conclusions that were being made.

We might reasonably suggest a further ethical principle of *anti-racism*, whereby psychologists are asked to ensure that their work is not racist and nor can it be used to cause racial offence.

REFLECTIVE EXERCISE 3.3

In a recent, real-life study that required ethical approval for a study with neuropsychological patients, the ethics committee refused to grant ethical permission because the study included only participants who were fluent in English, and this was considered discriminatory. The test materials had all been prepared in English and both memory performance and response time measures were being recorded to examine whether the patients had specific memory deficits. Despite the fact that someone who is not fluent in English would have performed poorly just because of their language skills, the ethics committee insisted that an interpreter should be provided for non-native speakers so that they would not be excluded. However, such participants would have produced performance data that would have had to have been discarded, and so to test them in the study would have been unethical.

Who sets the ethical agenda – the ethics committee that includes people who do not understand research, or the scientist who has been trained to consider major ethical issues in her or his research?

[From Robert Logie]

Sexism

Women have had a difficult job being recognized in psychology. The content of psychology has largely been concerned with male behavior and male experience, and academic psychology has created a number of barriers to the development and acceptance of its female colleagues.

In the content of psychology there has been a pervasive belittlement of women. If you look at the following quotes from famous male psychologists you will start to get the picture.

> We must start with the realisation that, as much as women want to be good scientists or engineers, they want first and foremost to be womanly companions of men and to be mothers.
>
> (Bruno Bettelheim, 1965, cited in Weisstein, 1992, p. 61)

> Much of a young woman's identity is already defined in her kind of attractiveness and in the selectivity of her search for the man (or men) by whom she wishes to be sought ...
>
> (Erik Erikson, 1964, cited in Weisstein, 1992, p. 62)

> Nor will you have escaped worrying about this problem – those of you who are men; to those of you who are women this will not apply – you are yourself the problem.
>
> (Sigmund Freud, 1973 [first published 1933], p. 146)

The above quotes are just a selection from a large sample of possible contributions. Women have largely been dealt with by psychology either as a problem or as the nurturers of children and men. It is fair to say that women's voices are now louder in psychology than they were, but the body of knowledge that is used as psychological evidence still requires an analysis that highlights its gender bias.

It is worth noting how many of the classic studies in psychology were largely carried out on male subjects. For example, two of the most cited studies on prejudice – Sherif's (1956) study of conflict and competition, and Tajfel's (1970) minimal group studies – were both carried out on boys. Kitzinger (1998) also points out that Erikson's model of identity across the lifespan is based on interviews with males, and Kohlberg's (1978) theory of moral development is based on a series of studies and interviews with males. The point is not that they just used boys but that the results were then applied to *people* in general – it was assumed that there are no gender differences.

We can argue for the inclusion of an ethical principle of *anti-sexism*, whereby psychologists seek to ensure that any bias or selectivity in their work is either acknowledged or reduced to a minimum.

We have picked out the two most written about 'isms' (racism and sexism) but clearly the list is endless (and includes speciesism, which is discussed in Chapter 5). The general principle is that people should not be categorized and degraded because of the perceived group they belong to, whether it is their ethnicity, their sex, their age, their nationality, their appearance, their physical abilities, their scout troup or whatever. This is a challenge for psychologists, who commonly use typologies to categorize people or use visible variables such as ethnicity or sex to look for differences in whatever quality they are measuring.

REFLECTIVE EXERCISE 3.4

In analyzing the results of a study funded by the federal government, you find a statistically different sex difference in the productivity of government employees who had been sent on a special management training course. Male employees who attended the course increased their productivity more than female employees. As a psychologist you have been asked to evaluate the effectiveness of the course, with no specific mention made of sex differences. You carried out an analysis of sex differences as a routine procedure. You feel an obligation to report the finding, but are concerned that reporting it might lead to women being less likely to attend the course in future. You believe this will happen no matter what interpretation is relayed in the research report, and wonder what the most ethical course of action would be.

[From Canadian Psychological Association et al., 2001]

The uses of psychological research

Science cannot detach itself from everyday life. You might only be interested in your scientific project and have no interest in politics or other murky things like that, but if you end up inventing the *pocket nuclear disintegrator gun* then this is not a good thing. It is unlikely that psychologists will invent a weapon of mass destruction, but they might well come up with theories or applications that will have a negative effect on large groups of people.

The apparently scientific issue of defining psychiatric conditions is a political battlefield. The decision to define a certain sort of behavior as pathological can have a major effect on people's lives. For example, homosexuality was once classified as a psychiatric condition, which, not surprisingly, led to very strong arguments around the *Diagnostic and Statistical Manual* (DSM) of the American Psychiatric Association.

Perhaps we can argue for an ethical principle to consider the *possible applications* of the research, both positive and negative, and to make efforts to reduce any of the possible negative uses.

Talking to the media

A professional hazard for psychologists is the insatiable thirst of the media for psychological analysis. On one level the information that psychologists give to media is an entertaining space-filler, but on another level it can have a major impact on the general public's view about events and about psychology.

We do not know about you, but the sight of psychologists on reality shows such as *Big Brother* (2000) commenting on whether a contestant fancies one of the other contestants based on observations of her body language makes us despair about psychology. Let us be clear about the limits of psychological knowledge – psychologists cannot read thoughts and cannot read intentions. It is not part of our training and not part of our expertise. The comments on *Big Brother* and similar program can be seen as amusing nonsense, but they cannot be regarded as scientific analysis. I would, therefore, like to propose a further ethical principle of *don't talk b*ll*cks to the media*. With regard to *Big Brother* and similar shows there is probably very little harm in it (although you may have a different opinion), but there are other examples that we will consider in Chapter 6 that have far graver consequences.

Using the principles and guidelines to judge research

Now that we have our principles, let us use them! Armed with my shield of ethical principles and my absolutist spear of truth, I can rip up virtually any piece of psychological research. This probably does not serve much real purpose but it might be useful in an essay when you are looking for an evaluative point. You need to be careful though. Let us have a look at two classic studies: the Milgram and Zimbardo studies. Milgram invariably appears in any list of unethical psychological studies but Zimbardo escapes with little blame. Is this fair?

Milgram was a good guy

If we go back to our four categories of ethics in Chapter 1 – consequences, actions, character and motives – then we might well argue that the *consequences* of Milgram's famous study are positive because it gives us a better understanding of evil and tyranny. His *motives* were sound because he was trying to answer questions about human behavior raised by activities in the Second World War (1939–1945). And we would say that he was a worthy *character* as evidenced by his writing and his other inventive and thought-provoking studies. The issue to consider is the *act* itself: the obedience study.

If we look at our ethical principles and guidelines then the important issues for this discussion are probably:

1 Informed consent and deception
2 Confidentiality
3 Protection of participants
4 Self-determination.

On the issue of **consent**, you could argue that the participants consented to the procedure and, in fact, volunteered for it. They did not know what the point of it was but they chose to do what they did. They were able to *withdraw* and about a third them did not complete the study, and they were *debriefed* at the end of the study. They were *deceived* about the focus of the study but it would not have worked without that deception. They were also deceived about the nature of the electric shocks, in that the 'learner' was only pretending to be

KEY TERM

Consent Giving your agreement to participate. A distinction is made between 'consent' and 'informed consent' where agreement is based on having comprehensive information concerning the nature and purpose of a study and the participant's role in it.

shocked. Mind you, this was probably a good thing as real shocks would have been more problematic (Milgram would have needed lots of confederates to be the 'learner').

The two that are harder to square are the issues of confidentiality and of protection from harm. The *confidentiality* of some of the participants has been compromised by the film footage of the study, although we might hope that consent for showing that material was given at the time and is still sought each time the tape is re-issued. On the issue of *protection from harm*, there is no doubt that the participants were subjected to an extremely stressful situation and that some had strong physical responses to it. It is this charge that tends to hang around the study, and that after the researchers had witnessed a number of extreme stress responses they could have chosen to terminate the study rather than continue it.

Milgram's defence was that he could not have known the outcome of the research before he started. Indeed, he asked psychiatrists how they expected people to behave in the study and they suggested that only a pathological minority would complete the study (which shows what they know!). Milgram (cited in Colman, 1987) further answered his critics by reporting the results of a follow-up survey of the subjects, carried out 1 year after the study. The results showed that 84% said they were glad to have been in the experiment and only 1.3% said they were very sorry to have been in the experiment. Milgram also described how the subjects had been examined by a psychiatrist one year after the study who was unable to find one subject who showed signs of long-term harm. There is a good argument to be made that the cost–benefit sheet on this study comes down in favor of Milgram.

Milgram did consider that he should stop the study:

> It became evident that some [subjects] would go to the end of the shock board, and some would experience stress. That point, it seems to me is the first legitimate junction at which one could even start to abandon the study. But momentary excitement is not the same as harm. As the experiment progressed there was no indication of injurious effects on the subjects; and as the subjects themselves strongly endorsed the experiment, the judgment I made was to continue the investigation.
>
> (Milgram, 1974, p. 212)

One final point to consider about the rights and wrongs of the Milgam study is that ethics are socially agreed rules. We noted in Chapter 1 that ethical principles vary with culture and time, so we can only judge people within the context of their culture and time. The ethical commit-tee of the American Psychological Association investigated Milgram's research not long after the first publication and eventually came to the conclusion that it was ethically acceptable, although Milgram's mem-bership was suspended while the committee deliberated the case. The American Association for the Advancement of Science awarded him a prize for outstanding contribution to social psychological research in 1965. In other words, Milgram's scientific peers considered the work and judged it to be ethical within their own criteria. So, by definition, Milgram's obedience study is ethical. We might not judge it the same way today, but it is not appropriate to judge Milgram badly when he was being accepted within the scientific community. If any judgement has to be made then it is against the whole scientific community and against psychology as an enterprise.

Zimbardo and the prison simulation studies

Another famous study already mentioned in this text is Zimbardo's prison simulation carried out at Stanford University in 1971. This study paid students to play the part of either guard or prisoner in a make-believe prison in the basement of the psychology department. Zimbardo was aware of Milgram's research and the ethical issues it raised and therefore tried to deal with these issues by seeking informed consent and warning participants about the procedures he was undertaking. However, despite his care, the experiment had to be stopped by Zimbardo after 6 days because of the deteriorating state of the prisoners and the increasing level of abuse by the guards. That is Zimbardo's story anyway, although it is worth noting that his girlfriend at the time of the study, Christina Maslach (subsequently Zimbardo's wife and currently professor of psychology at the University of California, Berkeley), went to see the study, was appalled at what she saw and ended up having a very big argument with Zimbardo. The study ended the next day. The power of love!

Like the obedience studies of Milgram, this work has been subjected to sustained attack by psychologists about its ethical nature. In Chapter 2 we looked at the charge from Haslam and Reicher (2003) that Zimbardo effectively encouraged brutal behavior by the guards, and we can add to that the issue of *protection from harm*, in that the prisoners were subjected to sustained degrading treatment. We can probably also raise issues of *consent* and *deception*, although like the obedience studies we might well be able to defend the experiment. The prison simulation has an extra and very damaging ethical problem, that of *withdrawal*.

There is video evidence of the prison simulation, although only a limited amount has ever been made available by Zimbardo for public scrutiny. On the bits available it is evident that the prisoners want to leave at one point. In fact one of the prisoners can be heard screaming 'I want out! I want out!'. In another harrowing segment where the prisoners are engaged in a physical struggle with the guards, a prisoner can be heard screaming 'F*** the experiment and f*** Zimbardo!', while another voice screams 'It's a f****** simulation'. The viewer has a clear impression that the prisoners want to get out of the study, and that they understand it is a role-play. This goes against Zimbardo's interpretation that the prisoners internalized the prison and believed in it, and that even when given the opportunity to leave they did not. In fact, Zimbardo refused to let the prisoners out after this outburst and gave them the impression that they could not get out. Zimbardo argues that the roles of guard and prisoner are so powerful that they override human judgement and basic decency. In fact, Zimbardo subsequently argued that his experiment was so disturbing, and unethical, that it should not be replicated. The upside of this for Zimbardo was that his results and interpretation could not be challenged.

The charges against Zimbardo are that he did not pay enough attention to protecting his participants from *harm*, and that he did not allow them the opportunity to *withdraw* even when they screamed to be allowed out. He also seems to contravene some other principles that do not fit our list above. First he took such an *active part* in the study that the result was contaminated by his own behavior and you might argue that the behavior in the prison was Zimbardo's creation. Second, by *misrepresenting* what went on and by arguing against any replication he gives a depressing and negative picture of human behavior that shows us as just doing what the situation demands of us without thought or moral choice.

This point is addressed by Haslam and Reicher (2003) when discussing their own prison simulation. They argue that Zimbardo's model of behavior and stranglehold on the empirical data perpetuates an injustice, in giving us such a negative and dispiriting view of human behavior. They believed they had an intellectual responsibility to challenge the evidence and a moral and political responsibility to challenge his view of people. One of the big problems was how to carry out a prison simulation study that was ethical. The result of their efforts was *The Experiment*, a four-part series broadcast on BBC television in 2002.

This work is worth a book in itself but our interest here is with the ethics of the replication study and how Haslam and Reicher were able to satisfy psychology colleagues and the BBC of its ethical nature. You can read about this on the BBC website and also at the SEORG site at Exeter University (see the end of the chapter). The report of the independent ethics panel is comprehensive and persuasive. The panel was chaired by an MP, and the credentials of the others are impressive (you can download the whole ethics report to check this out). The brief of the panel was to ensure the welfare of all the participants. They reviewed the plans for the study, which included being allowed to stop the filming at any point. During the filming there was 24-hour paramedic and security guard cover. Two clinical psychologists were on set from 7.30 a.m. to 11.00 p.m. every day, and available on call at other times.

Without doubt it can be argued that every effort was made to protect the prisoners from *harm*. They were also made aware that they could *withdraw* at any time. The tricky issue here is one of *consent* because they could not have known what was going to happen or how they would deal with this novel situation. But, as argued above about the obedience study, if we knew exactly what was going to happen there would be no point in doing the research. What did they find?

Unfortunately there is not enough space in this text to describe the results of *The Experiment*, although if we cut to the chase it provides a very strong challenge to Zimbardo's bleak picture of our behavior.

Are we making a fuss about nothing?

Do we get too upset about ethics? Look at the way people are treated in the many reality shows on prime-time TV. Surely it is OK to carry out psychology studies that wind people up a bit and trick them into unexpected behavior? We would argue not, and although we accept that it is probably not helpful to take an absolutist position, it is important to consider the cost–benefits of any ethical violation. There needs to be some benefit from the study other than providing entertainment for psychologists and the general public.

Summary

The BPS has a *Code of Ethics and Conduct* for psychologists. These provide useful guidance for practitioners and research-ers and are a useful tool for people who want to evaluate psy-chology. Looking back at some classic studies we can see that a robust argument can be made in defence of the Milgram obedience studies, although the Zimbardo prison simula-tion, in the opinion of the authors, is much harder to defend. Haslam and Reicher have shown that it is possible to carry out challenging studies within the bounds of ethical principles. But hey kids, don't do this at home!

FURTHER READING

- Blass, T. (2004) *The Man Who Shocked the World: The Life and Legacy of Stanley Milgram*. New York: Basic Books.
- Colman, A. (1987) *Facts, Fallacies and Frauds in Psychology*. London: HarperCollins.
- Miller, G. (1969) Psychology as a means of promoting human welfare. *American Psychologist, 24*, 1063–1075.
- Richards, G. (1998) The case of psychology and 'race'. *The Psychologist, 11*, 179–181.

WEBSITES

- British Psychological Society and ethics
  www.bps.org.uk/the-society/code-of-conduct/
- Milgram's research
  http://www.stanleymilgram.com/
  http://www.stanleymilgram.com/references.html
- SEORG The experiment (Haslam and Reicher)
  http://www.ex.ac.uk/Psychology/seorg/exp/
  http://news.bbc.co.uk/1/hi/entertainment/tv_and_radio/1779816.stm
- Zimbardo's research on the Stanford Prison Study (81 slides of the experiment)
  http://www.prisonexp.org/
- Zimbardo's discussion of the lessons and ethical issues raised by the prison experiment
  http://www.stanford.edu/dept/news/relaged/970108prisonexp.html

Psychological research with human participants

4

What this chapter will teach you

- Ethical issues are not just found in laboratory experiments
- Each different research method creates its own ethical issues
- Socially sensitive research creates special challenges

This chapter looks at a range of psychological studies, focusing in particular on the different methods that psychologists use to gather data, and gives some examples of the ethical issues that are posed by each method. We will also look at special kinds of research, such as research using the internet and socially sensitive research, and the ethical issues involved.

Laboratories and experiments

Much of the research that we have discussed so far has taken place in a laboratory setting and has been experimental. In fact many people equate laboratories and experiments with unethical practices. A scrubbed laboratory seems a place of potential torture, where the subject/participant is at the mercy of a highly manipulative experimenter. However, it is important to recognize that other kinds of research are equally prone to ethical problems. Furthermore it is important to recognize that laboratories and experiments do not necessarily go together. You can have an observational study conducted in a **laboratory**, or an **experiment** conducted outside the laboratory. For example, Zimbardo's study was in a laboratory but it was not an experiment. The study involved role-play and might be classed as a **controlled observation**. Controlled observations make use of laboratory environments in order to control important variables. For example, Ainsworth's Strange Situation (described on p. 25) involved recording infant behaviors in a very prescribed environment – the research room was a limited space (a 9 × 9 foot square) in order to prevent infants from wandering off. The space was divided into 16 smaller squares to help in recording the infant's movement. Bandura's well-known Bobo doll studies are another example of a controlled observation conducted in a laboratory – actually, an experiment that used controlled observation to measure the **dependent variable** if we want to be picky.

The argument is that merely placing a study in a laboratory does not make it unethical. Laboratories simply increase our ability to control variables, which is a necessary part of good research. Equally, a study using an experimental technique is not unethical because it is an experiment – what we want to focus on are the particular features in any study that raise ethical concerns.

KEY TERMS

Laboratory A specially constructed environment where conditions can be carefully controlled. It is also used for observational studies such as a study of sleep patterns.

Experiment A research method to investigate causal relationships by observing the effect of an independent variable on the dependent variable.

Controlled observation A form of investigation in which behavior is observed but under controlled conditions, as opposed to a naturalistic observation.

Dependent variable (DV) depends in some way on the independent variable (IV). The DV is measured in some way to assess the effects of the IV.

Field study Any study that is conducted outside a laboratory (i.e. not in a specially designed environment). This includes field experiments, naturalistic observations and case studies.

Field studies

Some **field studies** are experiments (such as Bickman's field experiment about obedience to authority, described on p. 37) but there are also field studies that are not experimental.

There are two key features of field studies that make them 'desirable' for understanding everyday human behavior. First, a field study is conducted in a relatively 'natural' environment so people are more likely to exhibit everyday behavior. But probably, most importantly, in most field studies the participants *do not know their behavior is being recorded* and this is the main reason why they exhibit everyday behavior. It is this aspect of field research that gives rise to ethical problems. It can be argued that this aspect of field research disregards their right to privacy and right to autonomy and respect.

A well-known example of a field study is the 'Good Samaritan' experiment by Piliavin *et al.* (1969). Psychology students boarded subway trains in New York city with the aim of seeing how passengers would respond to an emergency situation. A confederate faked some kind of collapse (either holding a bottle and smelling of alcohol or using a cane). The student observers took note of how long it took for help to be forthcoming.

What are the ethical issues here? There was no possibility of gaining prior consent, nor was it possible after the experiment to inform people about the study (i.e. debrief them). This challenges the participants' right to autonomy. In addition, participants might have experienced some psychological distress either from what they witnessed or their own feelings of self-doubt because they did not help. There would have been no opportunity to reassure them afterwards.

There is also the issue of privacy. A general rule (as we will see later) is that people should not be observed in a study unless it is in a public place, in other words one where they might expect to be observed by others. The subway setting would then not count as an invasion of privacy. According to this rule, the Good Samaritan study would be acceptable but the Tearoom Trade study (p. 28) would not.

The three ethical issues (consent, harm, privacy) discussed so far relate to participants' rights. Kimmel (1996) also points out that there are wider issues for the profession and society. Once such studies become general knowledge (and a number of psychological studies do make their way into the popular press), then people start to think that a person collapsing on the subway could just be a confederate in a psychology experiment. Such deceptions bring psychology into disrepute and may alter the behavior of the general public so, for example, they do not help in an emergency situation.

At their best, these studies give us an insight into how people behave in everyday situations; at their worse they are little more than a candid camera technique used to wind people up and then chuckle at their response.

Natural experiments

There are behaviors that psychologists wish to study but where it would be impossible to manipulate an **independent variable**, however such 'manipulation' may occur naturally. These are called **natural experiments** or **quasi-experiments**: for example, observing the effects of child abuse on emotional development or exposing individuals to TV and observing what effect this has on their behavior. You cannot deliberately expose a child to abuse for obvious reasons and you cannot deliberately stop people watching TV because there are

REFLECTIVE EXERCISE 4.1

In the 1940s and 1950s there was a lot of research looking at the effects of deprivation on infants. These were natural experiments where young children had been placed in an institution either because they were war orphans or because their families could not cope with them. More recently the issue of emotional deprivation is again being studied because of the opportunity sadly provided by events in Romania, where thousands of children were being cared for in orphanages because their families could not afford to look after them (the Ceausescu regime had banned abortion and contraception, leading to a large increase in birth rates).

In the UK many families have adopted these orphans, providing an opportunity for psychologists to study the effects of deprivation on social, emotional and cognitive development. Since the early 1990s the ERA Project has followed some of these children, comparing their development with that of a group of non-deprived adopted British children (Rutter et al., 2007). So far the children have been assessed at age 4, 6, 11 and 15 years, focusing on behavioral/emotional, cognitive, academic, social relationship and health outcomes (see the project website at www.iop.kcl.ac.uk/departments/?locator=750).

What ethical issues are raised by this natural experiment?

very few people in the world who have never watched TV. There are, however, some communities where TV has only recently been introduced, such as St. Helena (an island in the middle of the South Atlantic Ocean), and this gives psychologists the natural opportunity to observe the effects of TV (the independent variable) on, for example, antisocial behavior (a dependent variable) (Charlton et al., 2000).

What ethical issues arise from such research? It is usually possible to gain informed consent from participants but there are new problems. In the St. Helena study the presence of psychologists studying the community may have been intrusive and altered the behavior of participants. This could be seen as a form of psychological harm.

Privacy is also an issue with natural experiments, as with other kinds of research. Simply removing the names of individuals may be insufficient to ensure privacy because other details may identify the locality where the research took place, as in the case of the research on St. Helena. In such a study community members may easily be able to identify individuals.

Observational studies

We have already considered a few studies where observation was involved and ethically questioned. In the Tearoom Trade study there was total disregard for privacy and no consent was possible (see p. 27). As we noted, observing anyone in a public place may appear to be acceptable but it may also be important to consider what behaviors are being observed. For example, people may not think it an invasion of privacy to be observed in a park on a sunny day but might object if the observers' aim was to record instances of sexual activity (as in the Tearoom Trade study).

Some researchers have been interested in casual conversations. The obvious way to study this is to listen in on other people's conversations. Moore (1922) spent weeks walking round New York, writing down everything he heard and uncovering some interesting exchanges. In a more recent study Levin and Arluke (1985) made their record more impersonal by simply recording tone and focus. How would you feel if you found out that one of these studies had listened in to your conversation? Would you feel that this was an invasion of privacy (see Reflective Exercise 2.2)? Would you like to do the study yourself? Do you not do this as an amateur psychologist most days? Is there a difference between a formal study and informal observations? The same issues are raised in studies that observe behavior on the internet, for example taking note of what people say in online chat rooms. Such chat rooms are public arenas but is such observation acceptable? We will return to this later in the chapter.

A classic study by Festinger *et al.* (1956) involved participant observation, a technique where the observer is also a participant in the action. The aim of this study was to see how a group of people would respond when they found their beliefs threatened. A certain Mrs. Keech had a small but loyal following for her unusual religious beliefs. She predicted that the world was going to end on a certain day and gathered believers around her to witness the end of the world. Festinger and some colleagues infiltrated the group to see what happened. The world did not end and those present concluded that their faith had saved the world. There is little doubt that those present would have felt horrified if they knew there were imposters present and even more aggrieved if they knew the reason why. Of course other questions arise about how much the psychologists took part in the group activity and encouraged the behavior of Mrs. Keech. Did they, in fact, incite much of her behavior?

In the above studies the observations were **undisclosed (covert)**, in other words the individuals had no awareness that they were being watched or listened to, and did not know that such observations would be used for research purposes. In some studies observations are **disclosed (overt)** but there may still be ethical concerns. For example, the classic observation by Whyte (1943, described in Box 4.1) raises some interesting questions about the potential influence an observer may have on a group and the ethics of such interference. The same questions can be raised with respect to Rosenhan's (1973) study: *On Being Sane in Insane Places*. In the first part of this study participant observers ('pseudopatients') were admitted to mental hospitals because they claimed to be suffering from hallucinations. They then covertly watched and recorded the behavior of medical professionals in a mental institution. In the second part of the study the medical professionals knew their behavior was going to be observed – they were told that some pseudopatients

> **KEY TERM**
>
> **Undisclosed (covert) and disclosed (overt) observations** Observing people without their knowledge, for example using one-way mirrors or observing people with their knowledge, which may alter the way they behave.

> **BOX 4.1 Whyte's (1943) study of Italian street gangs**
>
> William Whyte wanted to find out what poor Italian families did with their money (he was an economist not a psychologist). To do this he decided to hang around the local street gangs, telling them that he was writing a book. Gradually he became assimilated into the group and inevitably the things he said and did had an effect on other group members, making them reflect on their own behavior.

might present themselves over the course of the next few months (in fact none did). Knowing their behavior was being observed led the medical professionals to behave differently from normal. Numerous ethical issues are raised here – deception, manipulation, possible psychological harm, from name but a few. Yet this was an overt naturalistic observation. Incidentally we are not aiming to criticize this study, which had an enormous, positive impact on our understanding of psychiatric diagnosis, merely to point out that the same problems that are usually associated with laboratory experiments do occur elsewhere.

> **REFLECTIVE EXERCISE 4.2**
>
> Use the four categories of ethics outlined in Chapter 1 (*consequences, actions, character* and *motives*) to assess the ethics of Rosenhan's study.

Questionnaire surveys

Questionnaire studies are very commonly used today because they provide a speedy way to collect data and relatively easy methods of analysis and comparison. It is estimated that about a third of all data in British psychology journals comes from questionnaire studies (Banyard & Hunt, 2000). The most common way to collect these data is through handing out questionnaire forms to students, often at the start of a lecture. It is not clear by how much the student is being coerced to take part (in the USA, such studies often form part of college course requirements), so there are sometimes issues of consent to consider (how easy would it be for a student to say no?). The questionnaire might also contain questions that could offend or cause distress, and this also has to be considered when reviewing the research.

A further ethical issue, in relation to questionnaire surveys, is how the data from the questionnaire are used. This issue will be discussed later in this chapter when considering socially sensitive research.

Research using correlational analysis

We often want to know the *cause* of events or behavior. Why did that happen, or why did you behave like that? We want reasons and causes. Experiments allow us to make inferences about what caused something because we have manipulated the variables and found out what effect they have. Correlational analysis, on the other hand, does not involve any manipulation and therefore we commonly say that we cannot infer cause from correlational data. This goes against our intuition and so we probably accept that smoking cigarettes *causes* cancer even though the evidence is correlational rather than experimental. To test this relationship experimentally we would have to take a number of non-smokers and randomly assign them to smoking and non-smoking groups, then come back in 20 years to see how many have developed cancer. As this research idea would never be acceptable we are stuck with correlational studies on such topics. The problem with the correlational evidence on smoking is that people who choose to smoke might be different from the people who choose not to smoke. In fact work by H.J. Eysenck (1991) (sponsored not surprisingly by the tobacco companies) found that if you remove differences in stress from the data then the cancer rates of smokers and non-smokers are not significantly different. This suggests that it is not smoking but in fact stress that causes cancer.

We intuitively believe in the coincidence of events. If two things happen together we tend to believe they are related. Just look at all the possible medicines and remedies there are on the market for all manner of health problems. Most health problems and psychiatric problems get better by themselves, given enough time, but if you take a remedy (hypothetically, Banyard and Flanagan's Magic Elixir of Life™: only three installments of £29.99 gets you a month's supply) then we can guarantee that most people will get better if they take it for a few weeks whatever they have. Many might come to believe that the Magic Elixir of Life™ is, in fact, magic and buy loads more of it. The real magic is the way that our bodies can heal us without us having to do anything. Mind you, we will not point that out because that would be bad for business and bad for all our fellow travelers on the untested and unproved medicine circuit – stand up homeopaths, counselors and astrologers. In case you think that comment is harsh, then try looking for studies on the effectiveness of any of those therapies.

The ethical issues that arise with correlational analyses come in the failure to fully explain the nature of the evidence. People have a tendency to attribute causal explanations to information that does not support their attributions (Heider, 1958), and researchers could be clearer about the limitations of their findings.

Having said that, the issue of causation is much more complicated than the simple distinction between the logic of experiments and correlations. Very little research in applied psychology is able to use experimental methods and commonly relies on regression analysis. Although this analysis does not allow us to make statements about what causes what, it does allow us to use our data to predict events and sometimes behavior.

KEY TERM

Regression analysis A technique used to calculate the equation that best describes the relationship between two or more variables. This equation can then be used to predict outcomes.

So, for example, with the smoking data we cannot say that smoking *causes* lung cancer and heart disease, but we can say that if you smoke there is *an increased probability* that you will get lung cancer or heart disease in later life. In other words, we can use the data about smoking to predict illness.

Case studies

In Chapter 1 we wrote about the **case study** of HM (see p. 3). It is actually not unusual for truly informed consent to be absent from a case study. One reason is that the case study method is often used with individuals who have impaired abilities because of the rarity value of such impairments – psychologists cannot launch larger scale studies because there are so few cases, so we look in detail at particular individuals. Genie (see p. 24) was a case study whose lack of social understanding and probable mental retardation made it impossible for her to provide informed consent. Genie was also young and therefore unable to give informed consent, a consideration that applies to many other well-known case studies (think of Little Hans and David Reimer – websites at the end of the chapter).

> **KEY TERM**
>
> **Case study** A research method that involves a detailed study of a single individual, institution or event, and usually involves a variety of different methods such as interviews and psychological tests.

Related to lack of informed consent, we have the question of invasion of privacy – if the individual has not consented to be studied, we are likely to be invading their privacy. Privacy refers to the zone of inaccessibility of body *or* mind and the trust that this will not be invaded. If privacy is invaded then confidentiality should be protected.

Consider the case of KG (Box 4.2), not really a psychological case study but a study quoted in most psychology textbooks. She certainly did not consent to the details of her life being revealed and we doubt whether she would wish to have been remembered in this way. She had family and friends and a full and interesting life. She was much more than a gruesome headline. This has led some people to argue that she should at the very least be accorded the respect given to HM or KF (another brain-damaged individual whose abilities informed our understanding of memory) and have some anonymity.

We live in an era where privacy is regularly invaded in pictures taken of movie stars and revelations about people's intimate lives. The psychological community is no exception and we constantly dig around for personal information about the 'stars' of psychological research. If you do search for KG on the web, you will find out lots of irrelevant

BOX 4.2   Murder in New York

KG arrived home at 3 a.m., after working in a bar all night. When she got out of the car she was approached by Winston Moseley, who stabbed her. She screamed and her cries were heard by several neighbors, but on a cold night with the windows closed only a few of them recognized the sound as a cry for help. When one of the neighbors shouted at the attacker, Moseley ran away and KG made her way towards her own apartment around the end of the building.

Moseley drove away but returned shortly afterwards and, following the trail of blood, found KG lying injured in the stairwell of her apartment, where he raped, robbed and finally murdered her. The time from the first assault until her death was about half an hour. The police were first called after she had actually died.

The case led psychologists to ask why no one had gone to her aid despite hearing her screams, a behavior described as 'bystander apathy'. The debate continues even today about the exact events of that night and how they might be interpreted.

information that is none of our business. You can also find out the true identity of Little Hans and information about where Genie is now. We are insatiable. But does that make it right?

One final ethical point to make about many of these case studies concerns what actually happens during the study. We have already described the incessant testing of HM (see p. 3) and the 'extreme, unreasonable, and outrageously intensive testing, experimentation, and observation' with Genie (see p. 25). Any individual in a case study will have spent hours, days, weeks and maybe even years being questioned and tested. This would seem to border on psychological harm.

Cross-cultural research

Cross-cultural research has given us a rich source of data about diverse groups of people and how they live. At its best it enhances our understanding and gives dignity to people who sometimes do not have a voice. As ever, though, not all examples of this research reach the highest levels of good practice and there are some ethical issues to deal with. Cross-cultural research is commonly conducted by Western psychologists and they bring to their research their own views of life and how it should be lived. It is impossible to be free from bias, so it is inevitable that some part of the researcher's views intrudes into the observations made of people. This is discussed further towards the end of this chapter when we consider socially sensitive issues such as culture.

In addition, the use of techniques developed in one culture and used in another (called **imposed etics**) may mean that comparisons made between cultural groups are not valid. For example, intelligence tests that were written and trialled with North American students may not be a fair test of intelligence among South Americans. To draw cross-cultural conclusions about intelligence using

> **KEY TERM**
>
> **Imposed etic** A technique or theory that is developed in one culture and then used to study the behavior of people in other cultures.

such tests may unfairly portray other cultures as inferior. This is an ethical issue, and also an example of socially sensitive research.

Another example can be seen in the work of Lawrence Kohlberg (1978) on moral development (described earlier on p. 17). He devised some moral dilemmas that draw out how people make decisions of right and wrong. He used these dilemmas in many parts of the world and found that children in different countries gave different responses to these dilemmas. He concluded that the most morally developed children in the world were American children from urban environments. He did not appear to take account of the fact that the dilemmas were devised in an urban American environment (Colby & Kohlberg, 1987).

In addition, it has been argued (Nobles, 1976) that Western re-searchers have plundered African people for knowledge and infor-mation in much the same way as European colonists plundered raw materials. Nobles argues that the data and the knowledge should be-long to the people who are the source of it. This would match up with the idea of seeing people as participants rather than subjects (see pp. 31–33).

Placebo studies

It is perhaps worth drawing attention to this particular kind of experi-mental research, which is used extensively when studing on the ef-fectiveness of psychological treatments. It is a topic that has attracted a lot of debate because on the one hand the method is scientifically

---

REFLECTIVE EXERCISE 4.3

You are a psychologist employed by a psychiatric hospital. You have particular expertise in treating depression, and have been asked to participate in clinical research that will compare the relative effects of two different medications against a placebo, in conjunction with and in the absence of cognitive therapy. Informed consent of clients will be a requirement for participation. When you point out that the research design will leave some research participants without any kind of treatment for 4 weeks, you are told this would not be a problem as it would be the same as being on a waiting list for treatment and, therefore, would not significantly disadvantage these clients. You are told that any participants in the control condition (placebo, no therapy) who become suicidal will be removed immediately from the study and receive treatment. Still, you feel uncomfortable with the design and worry about potential harm to clients in the control group.

What would you do?

[From Canadian Psychological Association *et al.*, 2001]

---

sound, but on the other it is ethically unsound. Typically a target group of patients are identified and then some are given a placebo treatment while others receive the real thing. This is likely to mean that some people receive an effective treatment while others do not. The dilemma is outlined in Reflective Exercise 4.3 (see above page).

Without a placebo group it may be difficult to assess effectiveness, but it can be done. For example two alternative treatments can be compared, or when a proven effective therapy exists this could be used as a control if there is evidence that the new therapy may be equally effective. In the 1990s the Canadian government's panel on research ethics declared that 'the use of placebos in clinical trials is generally unacceptable when standard therapies or interventions are available'. The important principle is equipoise: that participants in a research study should not be disadvantaged by their participation in research. The standard practice is to ensure that all participants are fully informed about all experimental conditions of a placebo

KEY TERMS

Placebo A dummy medical (or other) treatment given to assess the psychological effects of the treatment, i.e. the belief that the treatment is beneficial.

Equipoise An important principle in medical research, that there should be equal benefit offered in both experimental conditions (called 'arms') in a clinical trial.

study and informed that they will not know which condition they will be in. In other words, they agree that they potentially may receive a less effective treatment. This is akin to the method used by Gamson *et al.* (1982) (see p. 42) where participants essentially agreed to be deceived.

Internet-mediated research (IMR)

The advent of communication on the internet has created an almost limitless opportunity for psychologists to contact participants for research or to make use of existing data for their studies.

In terms of accessing participants through the internet, Nosek *et al.* (2002) identified three key differences between standard psychological research and research using the internet: the researcher is physically absent; informed consent and debriefing are problematic; and participant confidentiality is difficult to protect. Physical absence creates problems of trust. In cyberspace you could be anyone – this applies to both the researcher and the participant. The classic case of internet identity fraud was of a New York psychiatrist who wished to experience life from a woman's angle so he invented an internet persona called Joan, who described herself as a psychologist injured in a car accident. Joan became a major presence online and a support for 'other' disabled women (Van Gelder, 1985).

The second issue identified by Nosek *et al.* concerns informed consent and debriefing. In internet research participants who leave a study early cannot be adequately debriefed, although one possibility is to have a 'leave the study' button on every page of a questionnaire and if this is pressed offer debriefing to the respondent. The third issue is about confidentiality. In internet communications the researcher can trace the IP address of any respondent and so confidentiality cannot be protected. Some internet survey facilities such as *surveymonkey* routinely collect and report this information.

The internet also provides psychologists with rich, qualitative data generated in everyday lives. **Netnography** is a recently coined term to describe the use of information that has been made publicly available on the internet for research purposes, for example information on internet forums and chat rooms, both of which are considered to be public places (Kimmel, 2007). This raises questions similar to those already discussed with regard to observational studies – that it is not sufficient to consider whether a behavior

KEY TERM

Netnography (also called online ethnography) The use of material that is publically available on the internet for research purposes (often for consumer research). The term is derived from 'ethnography'.

REFLECTIVE EXERCISE 4.4

Thinking about internet research raises the question of the ethics of using publically available data without the individuals' consent. What are your views on the following dilemma, which a colleague shared with us:

There is a debate about how predictive A-level grades are of success in psychology degrees. One way to research this would be to make use of the application forms from hundreds of psychology graduates from all over the country applying to do a PGCE course. However, those applicants have not given permission for their data to be used in this way, so can I use it? I could of course seek the permission of all these applicants but most would not respond so I would be left with an unrepresentative sample, which negates the whole point of using the data. The issue here is of consent but it is also an example of where ethics can be simply a nuisance! It cannot harm those students and I get to see their grades anyway, so there are no privacy issues.

[From Matt Jarvis]

KEY TERM

Ethnography A method of participant observation used by sociologists and anthropologists to study daily life at first-hand.

is in public or not but it is also important to consider what behaviors are being observed. Another issue is that in traditional **ethnography** a key ethical principle is that the presence of the researcher is disclosed; this is more difficult in netnography but perhaps, more importantly, it is much easier not to be detected.

As yet no specific guidelines have been issued related to internet research except to assume that the same rules of respect, competence, autonomy and integrity apply here as much as anywhere in psychological research. The British Psychological Society (BPS) have published guidelines for internet-mediated research (British Psychological Society, 2009b) that are intended to supplement rather than replace the general ethical principles of the society. However, special note is made of the additional issues that arise from the most salient feature of internet research – the absence of physical contact between researcher and participant. The BPS recommends that research is carefully designed to ensure that participants are not unduly distressed in a situation where this might go unnoticed. The BPS also

---

REFLECTIVE EXERCISE 4.5

A student proposed that he would do a project on the efficacy of a yoga program that is marketed in India as a cure for homosexuality. He proposed that he would ask a gay friend to attend the course that was being run in London, document his experience and report on its effects on his homosexual behavior and feelings.

The student felt that any ethical objections should be balanced against the fact that the program ought to be discredited because it was not evidence based and promoted the idea that homosexuality was something that should be treated and 'cured'. Therefore the benefits should outweigh the costs.

What are your views?

[From Sara Meadows]

---

draws attention to the problem of deception (e.g. where researchers 'lurk' in chat rooms and record conversations) and suggests that there must be strong justifications for such research. From the researchers' point of view, they must be careful in verifying the identity of participants who may equally misrepresent themselves.

Socially sensitive research

All psychological research has a direct effect on individual people or on society in general, and if it does not then what is the point? Everything is a matter of degree, though, and at the far end of the spectrum we find research that might damage or offend people, such as Kohlberg's (1978) research that found that American children were more morally developed than children in other countries. Consider the potential consequences of this finding for Americans, who may therefore consider themselves superior, and for others, who would now see themselves as inferior. Sieber and Stanley defined socially sensitive research as:

> **KEY TERM**
>
> **Socially sensitive research** Any research that might have direct social consequences.

> Studies in which there are potential consequences or implications, either directly for the participants in the research or for the class of individuals represented by the research.
>
> (Sieber & Stanley, 1988, p. 49)

This definition is very broad and allows the inclusion of topics that are not commonly thought of as sensitive. It also alerts psychologists to their responsibilities to wider society. A recent (Halkitis *et al.,* 2003) piece of research into the behavior of gay men reported that some men were trying to infect themselves with AIDS (Triunfol, 2003). This behavior is referred to as barebacking or bug chasing. The research considered the complex motivations for this behavior but was criticized because it portrayed a negative image of gay men. The argument here is that the general public are likely to generalize to all gay men from the unusual examples of a few. There was no question about the quality of the research, only whether people should be told about it. The dilemma for researchers is whether to report what they find or whether to be more concerned with how the wider group is viewed.

Lee (1993) suggests that sensitive topics include areas that are private, stressful or sacred, or may expose stigmatizing or incriminating information. Research on the abuse of women and children may do both of these things and therefore have the potential to cause further pain and harm to individuals who are already experiencing abuse. It is not argued that these issues should be avoided but that the researchers should be fully prepared to deal with the likely effects of the research.

We (the authors) would argue that the teaching of socially sensitive issues such as anorexia can also raise serious ethical issues. If we are to believe the research into anorexia then it is likely that teachers deal every day with students who have such eating disorders. Anorexia nervosa is estimated to affect as many as 1 in 100 people (Matlin, 1987), although estimates of young women with mild versions of the disorder are as high as 10% (Brownell & Foreyt, 1986). Around 15% of women who are diagnosed as having anorexia nervosa die from the disorder, and under half regain a reasonable adjustment to eating. Teachers might well know the theory of eating disorders but are unlikely to be trained as counsellors to deal with the response they may get from vulnerable students. The problem is made worse by the expectation of many students that their psychology teacher has professional counseling skills as well as teaching skills.

Gender

Not all socially sensitive research concerns minority groups or troubled behavior. Take research on differences between men and women, which is one of the most commonly studied topics in psychology. If you

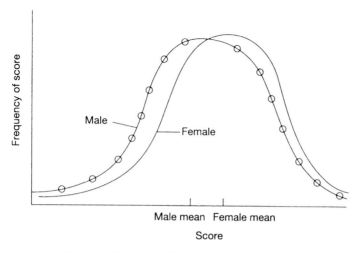

Figure 4.1 Distributions of binkiness in males and females

look at the average score of men on some dimension and compare it with the average score of women you commonly find a small difference. However, the spread of scores *within* men and women always far outweighs the *difference* between the two groups. Look at the example distributions in Figure 4.1, which show the different distributions of boys and girls on a made-up variable of 'binkiness'. You will see that girls have an average binkiness score a little higher than boys, but that the distributions overlap so much that it would be impossible to predict a person's binkiness score just by knowing their sex. Indeed, an analysis of the research on the development of social and cognitive behavior found that male–female difference accounted for only 1–5% of the variance in the population (Deaux, 1984). This means that sex is a very poor predictor of how an individual will behave.

The ethical problem here is that by using the easy-to-measure variable of sex, researchers tend to exaggerate the importance of that variable and give an unrealistic picture of how people can and do behave. The same can also be said for the even more controversial variable of race. Both of these are examples of socially sensitive research because such research has a social impact. Conclusions are reached that may not be valid, for example concluding that there are significant differences between men and women when the differences between the two sexes are very small in comparison to the differences within the sexes.

Cultural sensitivity

Cultural sensitivity refers to the understanding that enables us to gain access to individuals in society, to learn about their lifestyles and to communicate in ways that the individuals understand, believe, regard as relevant to themselves and are likely to act upon. Sieber argues that:

> Cultural sensitivity has nothing to do with the art and music of a culture, and almost everything to do with respect, shared decision making and effective communication. Too often, researchers ignore the values, the life-style and the cognitive and affective world of the subjects. They impose their own, perhaps in an attempt to reform people whose culture they would like to eradicate, or perhaps simply out of ignorance about the subjects reality.
>
> (Sieber, 1992, p. 129)

Being sensitive to other cultures is easier said than done. We are all affected by the bias of **ethnocentrism**. In our everyday lives we are asked to make judgements about people and events. We have a range of opinions that we are prepared to offer to other people when asked, and sometimes when not asked. In our judgements we are often inclined to show a little egocentrism (seeing things from our own particular viewpoint to the exclusion of others) or ethnocentrism (seeing things from the point of view of our group).

Ethnocentrism can be defined as the following syndrome of behaviors (LeVine & Campbell, 1972):

- a tendency to undervalue the outgroup's products
- an increased rejection and hostility towards outgroup members
- a tendency to overvalue the ingroup's products
- an increased liking for ingroup members (accompanied by pressures for conformity and group cohesion).

With an ethnocentric standpoint we tend to see our own team as being best. Also, we underestimate the errors and failings in our own team and exaggerate them in the opposing team. There are a number of reasons for this, including our access to evidence. We observe the behavior of people like ourselves because we mix with them, but we do not appear to mix outside our own groups very much. Recent reports (e.g. Ouseley, 2001) suggest that school playgrounds are becoming more segregated by ethnicity because children prefer the company of children from their own cultural communities. We are likely to know far more about the behavior and opinions of people we mix with and people who are like us. Also, if we support people like ourselves then we are likely to receive support back from these people. We expect our friends to support us and not to do us down, particularly in the company of strangers. It is all to do with social cohesion and a sense of belonging. The downside of the ethnocentric outlook is that we are likely to show *prejudice* towards people who are not like us and not in our group.

How does ethnocentrism intrude into psychology? Ethnocentrism means that we give undue prominence to our own group of people. In a fairly standard American text by Baron and Byrne (1991), 94% of the 1700 studies mentioned were in fact from America. In a British text (Hewstone *et al.*, 1988), about 66% of the studies were American, 32% were European and under 2% came from the rest of the world. These books are by no means exceptional, and they reflect the places where psychological research is conducted.

Research in psychology grew out of Europe and developed in America during the 20th century. Towards the end of that century in 1992 it was estimated that about two-thirds of research psychologists were from the USA (Smith & Bond, 1993) and this bias is reflected in the research areas that are still followed. The issue is even more complex than that because within British and American culture there is a range of ethnically diverse peoples, not all of whom are represented with psychology.

Things are changing, however, and over the last decade psychology has become much more international. It is estimated that there are over 1,000,000 psychologists worldwide now, of which around 300,000 come from Europe and a further 280,000 from the USA (Stevens & Gielen, 2007).

In 2002 the American Psychological Association (APA) published an extensive set of guidelines on multicultural research (see website at the end of this chapter). In the background material they note that the profession of psychology in the USA is not representative of peoples. Around 67% of the total population describe themselves as white, with the biggest other cultural groups being African-American and Hispanic, each of which account for 13% of the population. In psychology, however, if you look at people obtaining a first degree in psychology then only 10% are African-American and 10% are Hispanic. When it comes to doctorates then the figure for these two minority groups drops to 5%, and membership of the APA is only 2.1% Hispanic and 1.7% African-American.

The APA recognized that it has some issues to deal with around culture and ethnicity and developed a set of guidelines to help

BOX 4.3 *Guidelines on Multicultural Education, Training, Research, Practice, and Organizational Change for Psychologists* **(American Psychological Association, 2002a)**

Guideline 1: Psychologists are encouraged to recognize that, as cultural beings, they may hold attitudes and beliefs that can detrimentally influence their perceptions of and interactions with individuals who are ethnically and racially different from themselves.

Guideline 2: Psychologists are encouraged to recognize the importance of multicultural sensitivity/responsiveness, knowledge and understanding about ethnically and racially different individuals.

Guideline 3: As educators, psychologists are encouraged to employ the constructs of multiculturalism and diversity in psychological education.

Guideline 4: Culturally sensitive psychological researchers are encouraged to recognize the importance of conducting culture-centered and ethical psychological research among persons from ethnic, linguistic and racial minority backgrounds.

Guideline 5: Psychologists strive to apply culturally appropriate skills in clinical and other applied psychological practices.

Guideline 6: Psychologists are encouraged to use organizational change processes to support culturally informed organizational policy.

psychologists conduct culturally sensitive research. These are shown in Box 4.3.

Psychology can contribute to our understanding of people from different backgrounds from ourselves. It can add to our personal cultural sensitivity, but it can also contribute to cultural misunderstandings. Psychology has a long history of being associated with race science, which has sought to categorize people on the basis of their physical characteristics and to look for cognitive and behavioral differences. As mentioned earlier in this text about the intelligence debate (see p. 80), this enterprise is scientifically flawed and socially divisive (in the authors' view) because it emphasizes minor or non-existent differences between ethnic groups rather

KEY TERM

Race science commonly refers to the various attempts to cover racist ideas with a gloss of scientific respectability. The science is invariably poor and the conclusions are racist.

than the many values, behaviors and ambitions that they share. This is not to say that there are no scientific questions to ask about this issue, but if it is virtually impossible to define race (Jones, 1991; see also Chapter 2) and very difficult to find comparable samples in different cultures, then the conclusions that will be drawn from the research will be open to much question and debate.

Should socially sensitive research be avoided?

So, where does this leave us? Well if you want an easy life, do not do or study socially sensitive research, but is this an option? Sieber and Stanley clearly do not think so, and write:

> Sensitive research addresses some of society's pressing social issues and policy questions. Although ignoring the ethical issues in sensitive research is not a responsible approach to science, shying away from controversial topics, simply because they are controversial, is also an avoidance of responsibility.
>
> (Sieber & Stanley, 1988, p. 55)

One of the ethical issues that can arise with socially sensitive research is that the participants might be vulnerable and distressed or might have a number of unresolved conflicts, and therefore might not be fully in control of the interview. In the research process the skilled researcher may extract more information from the participant that she or he intended to disclose (Sieber & Stanley, 1988). The interviewer may have developed their skills over a number of years and know how to get to the heart of the story, and the participant may be disclosing this information for the first time so will not have rehearsed the story or thought through the implications of telling it.

An example of the problem is described by Edwards (1993) after she had interviewed 31 mothers about their experience of being a student in higher education. She writes:

> ... some of the women I talked to were either in, or close to, tears during parts of their interviews and certainly I found this disturbing and wondered what on earth I was doing to them and to me.
>
> (Edwards, 1993, p. 193)

You might argue that initiating a conversation that leads the other person to tears is ethically wrong, but is this necessarily so? When we talk about things or events that mean a lot to us we can become emotional. If we argue that researchers should avoid emotional topics we would exclude some of the most important issues from psychological research. It does not seem appropriate to use the criteria of emotions ('did they cry?') as to whether research is ethical or not, but neither is it appropriate to completely ignore them.

Another example of a sensitive issue is the false memory/recovered memory debate (see also Chapter 2). Over the past 20 years the famous memory psychologist Elizabeth Loftus has written about the validity of 'recovered memories' of childhood abuse, despite personal and professional threats. These memories commonly come to light only after therapeutic sessions with people who use techniques such as guided imagery to explore early life experiences. Until the therapy, the clients had been unaware of any abuse as a child. Loftus' work with experimental memory studies, as well as through legal work, has led to the our increased understanding that, even though these 'memories' appear to be very believable, they are often the result of recent reconstructive processes rather than of past events. In other words, the 'remembered' events did not happen. She was awarded the William James Fellow Award of the American Psychological Society (APS) in 2001 for this work, and her citation commented that:

> ... Dr. Loftus has joined the ranks of other scientists, past and present, who have had the courage, inspiration, and inner strength to weather the widespread scorn and oppression that unfortunately but inevitably accompanies clear and compelling scientific data that have the effrontery to fly in the face of dearly held belief.

The work of Loftus, among others, has done much to calm down the more extravagant claims around the issues of false memories and child abuse. This is not to say that false memories and child abuse do not occur, but just that they do not occur as commonly as suggested. Also it is important to say that abused children often do not report the abuse for many years, but this is not the same as never knowing you were abused until you are taken through some guided imagery by someone who specializes in recovering memories of child abuse.

There has been a rash of lawsuits in America by patients who were led to believe, during therapy, that they had repressed memories that were the result of child abuse, and later came to realize that none of this was true. A major damages payout went to Patricia Burgus, one of the first patients admitted to the **Dissociative Disorders** Unit of a major Chicago hospital. She was given six years of treatment, including hypnosis and powerful medication, and at one point became convinced that she had over 300 different personalities that were supposed to be a direct result of extended childhood abuse. Burgus believed she had experienced cannibalism, ritual murder and torture at the hands of her own family. Her two young sons were also hospitalized for years on the dubious theory that dissociative disorder

KEY TERM

Dissociative disorders Mental disorders where the patient experiences dissociation from or interruption of 'normal' of waking functions such memory (amnesia) or identity (multiple personality disorder, now called dissociative identity disorder, where a person has multiple identities).

tends to be genetically based. When Burgus finally realised that her memories were untrue, she went to court where she and her family received a $10.6 million settlement (Loftus, 2000).

So should psychologists conduct socially sensitive research? Many psychologists might feel that they would prefer to avoid difficult and sensitive work for fear of getting it wrong, and as a result vulnerable and distressed people might not receive valuable support. But if you offer that support and get it badly wrong you might end up doing more harm than good. It is a tough call.

Students often want to conduct research that is socially sensitive, for example on eating disorders or homosexuality. Perhaps this just shows us that many of the topics that really interest us are socially sensitive ones. Important issues are often sensitive issues and that is what makes them important. It is not surprising, therefore, that psychologists sometimes upset or challenge people. Socially sensitive research is likely to be distressing to the participants, the researchers and also to those who have to deal with the information.

Summary

Ethical problems are not confined to laboratories or experiments in psychology. The common stereotype of the laboratory experiment as being ethically dubious and all other methods being ethical sound is incorrect. Every data collection technique and every location presents its own ethical challenges, and it is necessary to return to the principles of good practice when conducting any research. This is especially important as new technologies present new methods of conducting research, such as netnography. Research that has important social implications should not be shied away from but must be treated with great sensitivity.

FURTHER READING

- Sieber, J. E. & Stanley, B. (1988). Ethical and professional dimensions of socially sensitive research. *American Psychologist*, *43*, 49–55. [The original article that sparked off much of the thinking about socially sensitive research; it discusses the issues as well as ways of dealing with them.]

WEBSITES

- APA guidelines on multicultural research
  http://www.apa.org/pi/oema/resources/policy/multicultural-guidelines.aspx
- BPS Report of the working party on conducting research on the internet
  http://www.admin.ox.ac.uk/curec/internetresearch.pdf
- David Reimer
  http://www.cbc.ca/news/background/reimer/
  http://www.slate.com/id/2101678/
- Genie
  www.feralchildren.com/en/showchild.php?ch=genie
- Internet-mediated research (an up-to-date listing of current projects)
  http://psych.hanover.edu/Research/exponnet.html
- Little Hans (see the end of the story)
  http://en.wikipedia.org/wiki/Herbert_Graf
- NY Aids Coalition
  www.nyaidscoalition.org
- St. Helena project
  http://website.lineone.net/~sthelena/
  http://www.glos.ac.uk/education/content.asp?sid=4

Psychological research with animals

5

What this chapter will teach you

- How animals have been used in psychological research

- The law regarding the use of animals and relevant 'codes of practice'

- Scientific arguments for and against the value of using animals to increase psychological knowledge

- Ethical arguments for and against using animals in research

---

This chapter turns our attention to the issue of using non-human animals in psychological research. There are two questions to ask: To what extent is research with animals *valuable*? And to what extent is it *acceptable* or ethical? In other words, in this chapter we are not just concerned with ethics but also with the questions of whether such research is useful or necessary.

One thing to bear in mind as you read this chapter is that we are concerned with *psychological* research. Websites about animal rights are often concerned with factory farming and cosmetic research, so it

Figure 5.1 Pictures of cuddly animals are used to evoke an emotional response against the use of non-human animals in research

is important to remember that our *focus* is on psychological research – although this does overlap to some extent with medical research, for example when testing drugs to treat mental disorders.

Emotion and flawed logic

No one is suggesting that animal research should be undertaken lightly but it is important to approach the topic dispassionately and logically, looking for facts rather than unsupported claims, and looking at the balance between costs and benefits, as with all ethical issues.

This chapter starts with a review of the use of non-human animals in psychological research just to give you a platform for thinking about this kind of research. Next we review constraints that are currently in place to govern the use of animals, and finally we turn to questions of usefulness (whether the research is scientifically valuable) and ethics (whether the research is morally acceptable).

Examples of research with non-human animals

The best place to begin our dispassionate considerations is to look at the kind of research that is conducted by psychologists. When thinking of animal research you may have a mental image of dogs pinned down to dissection tables. Cast such images from your mind.

We are concerned with psychological research and very little psychological research involves operating theaters or surgery. However, this is not to suggest that psychological research is relatively harmless. Psychologists have developed their own brands of unethical research, as we will see. The sorts of issues that will concern us are not just whether an animal is harmed during the research process itself but also whether an animal's behavior or physiology is affected by the research procedures in such a way that the animal's subsequent life is altered. We are also concerned with the care of animals before, during and after they are participants in research. It is not just the procedures performed by a psychologist but the general care of the research participant.

Harlow's monkeys

A very well-known series of experiments was led by Harry Harlow in the 1950s. His early research on learning with rhesus monkeys led him to breed his own monkeys in captivity in order to improve their survival rates. The monkeys were brought up in separate cages to reduce the chances of infection and they developed a number of unusual and damaging behaviors that are not commonly observed in animals. The striking thing to the observers was that the behaviors, such as repetitive movements, rocking and self-injury, are commonly seen in disturbed humans. Harlow noticed that when he released his isolated monkeys from their individual cages they were unable to get on with other monkeys and appeared unable to develop normal social relationships or even to mate.

This disturbed and damaging behavior developed from the attempt to reduce the chances of disease and was not anticipated by Harlow (1959). As such it would be hard to criticize him and his research team for unethical conduct. There is a problem, however, with what happened next. Having found that isolation had a damaging effect on monkeys he then set out to investigate this by deliberately creating disturbed monkeys through further isolation experiments. Among the popularly recorded findings are that his orphan monkeys became very attached to the cloth nappies used to line their cage. This led him to investigate the hypothesis that young animals seek contact-comfort. He did this through a series of experiments involving monkeys and two wire 'mothers' – one covered in cloth and the other with no cloth but a feeding bottle (Figure 5.2). The monkeys showed a surprising preference for the cloth mothers, demonstrating the importance of contact-comfort in attachment. This demonstrated the

Figure 5.2 Harlow demonstrated the importance of contact-comfort in emotional development by raising rhesus monkeys with 'wire mothers'. The monkeys preferred the cloth-covered 'mother', demonstrating the importance of contact-comfort in emotional development. However, these monkeys suffered lifelong damage as they remained emotionally maladjusted, presumably due to the lack of reciprocal affection from their 'mother'. Reprinted from *Behavioral Biology, 12*, Harlow, H.F. and Suomi, S.J., Induced depression in monkeys, 273–296, 1974, with permission from Elsevier

importance of reciprocal attachment for healthy emotional development because these monkeys, 'raised' by an unresponsive mother, became quite disturbed adults.

Harlow's work is sometimes justified as providing a valuable insight into the development of attachment and social behavior. At the time of the research there was a dominant belief that attachment was related to physical rather than emotional care. It was the fashion in parts of American society for adults to be remote from children and not be very affectionate. The theoretical work of John Bowlby and others, such as Robert Hinde, challenged such views and Harlow's (1959) research was used as empirical support for these theories. It is arguable as to how important this research evidence was. It may be that it was totally unnecessary (there was also research with human infants) or it may actually have been vital in convincing people about the importance of emotional care in hospitals, children's homes and child care generally.

Harlow's depression studies

You may feel that the benefit of Harlow's early research justifies the permanent damage done to his subjects, but this is probably not the case with his subsequent research, which was again with rhesus monkeys. Harlow himself suffered long spells of depression and therefore was interested in studying factors that might cause depression. He started with social isolation experiments, where rhesus monkeys were placed in a cage for 30 days. The monkeys saw nothing except the experimenter's hands when the food and water were being changed. At the end of the study the monkeys were so disturbed that two of them refused to eat and starved to death. In the subsequent experiments the monkeys were force-fed so they would survive and their behavior could be observed. Harlow isolated monkeys for six months and then for an entire year. The effect was to create a monkey who barely moved and did not play, or explore; in short, the monkey was chronically depressed.

Harlow remained relentless in his search to understand the origins of depression. Next he created a 'vertical chamber apparatus' (Figure 5.3). Monkeys were kept in this apparatus for a month. They were all 'normal' before they entered the 'pit', but within a short while they appeared to give up and would sit hunched in a corner at the bottom of the apparatus. Once 'released' they remained withdrawn and emotionally damaged, which was not really very surprising. The experiments were widely condemned:

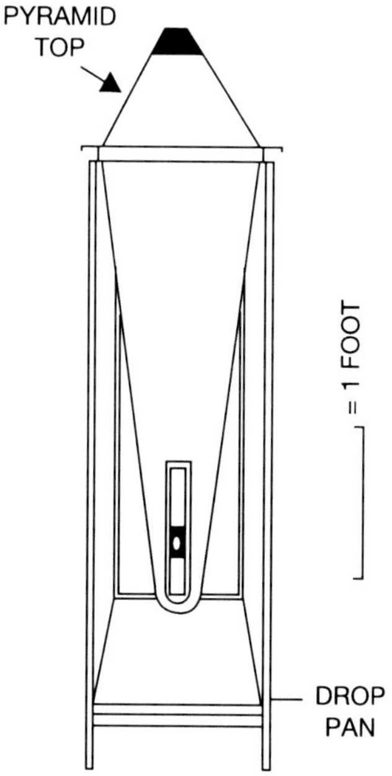

Figure 5.3 The vertical chamber apparatus was a V-shaped stainless-steel container with sloping sides and a rounded bottom. There was a mesh floor about an inch above the bottom of the container that allowed waste material to drop through the drain and out of holes drilled in the stainless-steel. The chamber was equipped with a food box and a water-bottle holder, and was covered with a pyramid top, designed to discourage incarcerated subjects from hanging from the upper part of the chamber

Harry Harlow and his colleagues go on torturing their nonhuman primates decade after decade, invariably proving what we all knew in advance – that social creatures can be destroyed by destroying their social ties. His most recent outrage consists of placing monkeys in 'solitary' for twenty days – what he calls a 'vertical chamber apparatus ... designed on an intuitive basis' to produce 'a state of helplessness and hopelessness, sunken in a well of despair.

(Booth, 1974, p. 114)

Operant training

B.F. Skinner conducted a large number of laboratory experiments to demonstrate the principles and application of operant conditioning. For example, a rat would be placed in a box with a lever, and if the lever was pressed a pellet of food was delivered. This acted as a reinforcer and the rat acquired a new behavior. This all sounds quite jolly and the rat appears to be having the life of Riley, sat around all day in a cosy box just pressing levers for food. Sadly, it was not all joy for the rats even when it appeared so.

The work of Olds and Milner (1954) is an illustration of this. They were interested in what makes something pleasurable. We find things like food, drink or sex pleasurable, but why? What is pleasure? They investigated this using rats in a Skinner Box. Instead of getting food when they pressed the lever, the rats received a brief electric shock to the brain through a small wire implanted in their heads. You would imagine that an electrical current to the brain would be very unpleasant, in which case the rat would press the lever only once or twice before

---

REFLECTIVE EXERCISE 5.1

You are a psychology professor and have received a call at home early on Saturday morning informing you that the furnace in the building that houses your rats has broken down and will not be operational for at least 48 hours. Realizing that the rats are likely to die due to the 30° temperature outside, you decide to go to the university and bring the animals home for the weekend. However, you cannot get your car started. After making a few phone calls to explore other means of getting there, you realize that your only alternative is to get a taxi. The return taxi trip will cost you £200. Considering the fact that the study in which the rats were being used is finished and the rats are due to be destroyed the following Tuesday anyway, you wonder if it is worth it.

What would you recommend?

[From Canadian Psychological Association *et al.*, 2001]

scuttling off to the other side of the cage as far away from the lever as possible. This was not, however, the outcome of the study.

The results show that the rats continued to press the lever when the wire was in the septal area of their brains. In other words, they chose to give themselves electrical stimulation when given the opportunity. They spent, on average, 85% of their time regularly pressing the lever to obtain the stimulation. One rat stimulated itself with lever presses over 7500 times in 12 hours at an average of 742 responses an hour, or more than once every 5 seconds. We have to conclude that the lever pressing, and hence the stimulation, was very reinforcing. Before you start thinking to yourself that you would like to be connected up to something that seems so much fun, it is worth pointing out that the rats paid a price for this fun. Olds and Milner report that 'after testing the animal was sacrificed' (p. 419), and its brain was examined to find the exact location of the electrode.

The ethical judgement centers around whether you think this work provides valuable insights that will have tangible benefits. If you think the work of the behaviorists has scientific and social merit then the use of animals is justifiable and possibly ethical, but if you do not accept the scientific merit of the work then the ethical justification becomes harder to make.

It is also worth noting that when we talk about laboratory rats we are not referring to the friendly rat at the bottom of your garden or in your cellar. This wild rat is a lively little chap capable of spectacularly quick learning, as well as transporting some of the most deadly diseases the world has ever known (plague, botulism, etc.) The laboratory rat is an altogether different animal. They have been selectively bred over many generations for their docility and their ability to deal with the laboratory environment. They would not survive for long if they were released in the gardens and cellars of Britain. This adds a further question mark over the work because we are looking at the behavior of a manufactured species in a manufactured environment and trying to apply it to real-life problems.

Sensory deprivation

One technique used to investigate development is to deprive an animal (or person) of part of its normal experience and see what the long-term consequences are. It is argued that this technique allows us to investigate the relative effects of genetics and learning in any behavior. The work of Harlow (above) can be seen as a deprivation design in that the animals were deprived of normal social and even physical contact. This technique has been extensively used in the study of perception.

Some of the earliest studies of this type investigated what happens to an animal if it is brought up without any visual stimulation – in other words, in the dark. The point of these studies was to find out whether the animals had to learn to see from scratch when finally they were brought into the light or whether they would have some innate visual abilities that were unaffected by experience. Studies by Riesen (1956), for example, found that cats, chimpanzees and other animals did not develop their full visual abilities while being raised in total darkness. In fact the experience left them unable to ever see properly in their lives. Light deprivation seems to have severe effects on the perceptual system, and this occurs even if the deprivation is only in one eye. Hubel *et al.* (1977) surgically closed one eye of 2-week-old monkeys and found that their visual systems subsequently did not develop normally.

A refinement on the sensory deprivation technique is to provide restricted stimulation rather than no stimulation. A particularly famous study was conducted on kittens in restricted environments (Blakemore & Cooper, 1970). In one of these studies the kittens only had early experience of either vertical or horizontal lines rather than a full visual world. When tested after 5 months of living in this restricted environment they were able to get around normally but were virtually blind to lines that were perpendicular to those they had been exposed

---

REFLECTIVE EXERCISE 5.2

Is there too much animal research in the UK? See Figures 5.4 and 5.5 and consider the list below.

- In 2008 there were just under 3.7 million scientific procedures using animals (Home Office data) but the annual number of animal experiments is no higher than it was 20 years ago.
- Recent rises in animal experiments are due to the use of genetically altered animals (mostly mice and fish), which now make up half of all animals used.
- UK bioscience and medical research funding more than doubled in real terms in the decade to 2008, but animal procedures rose by just one third.

But remember – most of this research are not psychological. Data about psychological research are not kept separately.

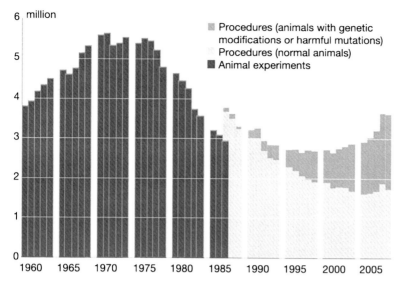

Figure 5.4 Animal experiments in the UK, 1975–2009. Data source: Home Office; graph courtesy of Understanding Animal Research

to in their restricted environment (i.e. the kittens raised with vertical lines often tripped over strings stretched between two chairs – a horizontal line).

You might well ask why a zoo-full of animals and birds has been blinded and deafened, but the scientist might well argue that there has been some benefit in our knowledge of sensory processes and therefore our treatment of people with sensory deficits (as we will see later). Other work by Hubel and Wiesel (1962) discovered the areas of the brain responsible for perceiving the orientation of lines, and this work brought them a Nobel Prize. It is easy to be critical of all animal research but before you dismiss it out of hand it is important to weigh up the possible benefits of these studies.

Field studies

We should also consider research conducted in more natural environments. For example, Gardner and Gardner (1969) raised a chimpanzee called Washoe in their own home and taught her to use sign language, achieving a reasonable degree of success. The reason for training the chimpanzee in a home environment was so that the animal could acquire language as children do – as part of everyday life. This means that the chimpanzees were enculturated into human society

BOX 5.1   Which animals are used?

Chimpanzees, orang-utans and gorillas have not been used in the UK for over 20 years and their use is now banned. Other primates and monkeys can still be used but this is rare. Home Office statistics show the following division of species in recent research in the UK.

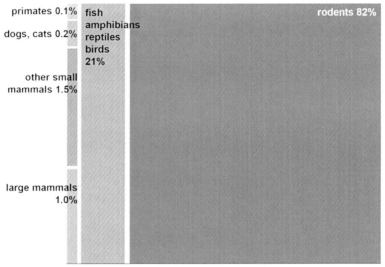

Types of animals by percentage, 2009

Figure 5.5 Distribution of animal species used for research in the UK. Data source: Home Office; graph courtesy of Understanding Animal Research

and removed from their natural lifestyle and culture. This is a big issue because Washoe passed on what she learned to her adopted child. The researchers are potentially creating a whole new society.

When such investigations are over, researchers have a duty to provide lifelong care for these primates. In the case of Washoe and her comrades they actually did this (see website at the end of this chapter). However, not all primates used in psychological research have been so lucky, although there are a number of facilities that provide care for animals once research projects are finished.

We might also consider another well-known field study that concerned animal communication. Seyfarth and Cheney (1980) demonstrated how vervet monkeys use different alarm calls. They did this by recording the monkeys' calls in response to different predators and playing these back to other monkeys to demonstrate that different calls had specific meanings. The effect may be that monkeys hearing such calls in the absence of any predator may learn not to respond. This could endanger their lives in the future if they fail to respond to alarm calls involving real predators.

Naturalistic observations

It is important to remember that there are a number of studies conducted on animal behavior that are purely observational and involve no interference with the animals being studied. Ethologists seek to study animals in a way that does not affect their behavior – For example, Dian Fossey's work observing gorillas in the natural habitat to reach a greater understanding of their social relationships, made famous through the film 'Gorillas in the Mist'.

However, psychological research does tend to be more of the investigational variety, where some variables have been manipulated to observe the effects on behavior and such manipulations raise ethical concerns.

Drug and addiction research

The research area that has probably raised the greatest number of ethical concerns is drug testing. Psychologists and psychiatrists have a great interest in the use and safety of medication for mental disorders and, as such, the research testing these drugs constitutes psychological research. A considerable amount is written about the way animals are used in such research, for example one website against the use of animals states that:

> drug companies [test] numerous experimental medications, killing millions of animals every year. Animals in these laboratories spend their short lives locked in cages, given test drugs, observed, killed and dissected. If painful side effects are noticed, they are logged and nothing more; to administer pain relief would be interfering with the study.

> (www.askuswhy.com)

It is worth mentioning that such descriptions are often inflammatory – note, for example, the mention of dissection; if an animal is dissected it is dead, so that really is not an issue. However, it is indisputable that

REFLECTIVE EXERCISE 5.3

In March 2006 six volunteers were injected with a drug that was being tested for use with multiple sclerosis. The drug had been tested, with no ill effects, on mice, rats, rabbits and monkeys. Within minutes of receiving the injection the volunteers were writhing on the floor and two suffered permanent organ damage. Some people argue that this shows that animal testing is a waste of time.

What are your views?

drugs can cause animal suffering and distress but, it is argued, this is balanced against the potential benefits for humans. For example, the advent of drug therapies for mental illnesses in the 1950s significantly reduced the number of people incarcerated in mental institutions and psychoactive drugs continue to allow people with mental illnesses to lead relatively 'normal' lives (protecting them and protecting society).

Related to drug research is research on the addictive properties of drugs. Animals are often used in this research in order to observe the effects of repeated doses of drugs on physiology and behavior. Take one randomly select study as an example – a recent study using rhesus monkeys to show that amphetamines could be used to treat cocaine addiction (Martelle *et al.*, 2008). Cocaine addictions were created in the monkeys and the strength of this addiction was demonstrated by getting them to press a lever as many as 1000 times in order to get their injection. They were then given amphetamine for 24 hours and a week later cocaine use was reduced by about 60%. There is no doubt that drug addiction is a major human problem but creating even more addicts, albeit animals, may not be the solution. In this particular study the researchers commented that the study supported what had been observed in humans.

Genetic inheritance

The final area of research that we are going to review is where animals are bred to enhance or reduce certain characteristics. Such research can give very useful insights into the issue of nature versus nurture, for instance in understanding the role of genetic factors in the success of certain drug therapies. Solberg *et al.* (2006) have spent decades breeding rats who are severely depressed (mating depressed rats with depressed rats, so that you get rats 'who are believed to be the most depressed rats in the world'). This meant that the research team could identify genes linked to depression. Next they exposed a different group of rats to stressful situations for two weeks so that they could select the rats that did not cope well and identify the genes linked to this poor stress response. The big news was that there was no overlap between the depression genes (in the most depressed rats in the world) and the stress genes. This suggests that the idea that stress causes depression may be wrong and may explain why anti-depressants are often ineffective – antidepressants treat stress, and therefore only work in people suffering from stress *and* depression, not those who are just depressed. You may ask whether this research is relevant to humans, but the researchers claim that rat brains are very similar to human brains so it is reasonable to draw analogies and potentially is very useful work.

The problem with such research is that it treats animals as renewable resources and this is a major issue from the ethical viewpoint. Is it acceptable for humans to farm rats in the same way that they might farm trees, by simply re-growing them as and when the need requires?

Commentary

This review of research may leave you feeling dismayed by the kinds of things that psychologists have done and are continuing to do in the name of understanding human behavior. However, much of it is quite old and research such as Harlow's would not be conducted today. This is undoubtedly due to the objections raised by Animal Rights Movements, which have increased sensitivities about the use of animals in research and have also led to increasingly stringent laws related to animal research, the topic we turn to next.

Regulation of animal research

Research using animals is regulated in two ways – by laws and by professional guidance.

Legislation

Individual countries produce their own laws regarding the use of animals in research. The UK was the first country in the world to protect research animals, through a law in 1876. This was introduced even before there were any laws to protect children. In fact, ironically, the first case of child abuse that was ever brought to court relied on legislation for the protection of animals. In the 1870s a nine-year-old child, Mary Ellen Wilson, had been beaten, cut and burned by her foster mother for more than seven years. A concerned social worker made appeals to police, the church and the courts, but with no success. As a last resort she turned to the American Society for the Prevention of Cruelty to Animals. They brought Mary Ellen's case to court, arguing that she was a member of the animal kingdom and therefore deserved the same protection (Shelman & Lazoritz, 1999). At the time there were laws protecting animals but no laws protecting children. So there is a longer history of protection of animals than children.

In the UK the 1876 act was finally revised with the current law, the Animals (Scientific Procedures) Act (1986); the key points are identified in Box 5.2. This act aims to safeguard laboratory animal welfare while allowing important medical research to continue – it balances costs and benefits. These controls are widely regarded as the strictest in the world (House of Lords Select Committee on Animals, 2002) and failure to comply with the law will lead to prosecution and possible custodial sentences. [Note that a current European directive (September 2010) on animal use in scientific procedures means that UK law will be amended.]

There are other laws that are relevant to the animal research debate, most particularly the laws relating to the licensing of new drugs. Before a drug can be tested on human volunteers it must be used with at least

---

BOX 5.2 The Animals (Scientific Procedures) Act (1986)

1 The act relates only to vertebrate animals and only to those more than halfway through their gestation period. One invertebrate species (the octopus) was added in 1993. Primates, cats, dogs and horses have additional protection.
2 Research can only be carried out if a Home Office license is granted to the person, the project and the place of research. Thus there are three 'levels' of regulation, all of which require a separate license.
3 When considering costs versus benefits, investigators must decide whether the knowledge to be gained from any investigation justifies harm or distress to animal participants. This also influences the granting of licenses.

two different species of live mammal, one of which must be a large non-rodent. This means that mammals must be used in drug research.

The principle of the 3Rs

In 2000, the Home Office issued further guidance on the operation of the 1986 Act. In particular this introduced the guiding principle of the 3Rs, first proposed by Russell and Burch in 1959. The recent Home Office guidance, paragraph 2.3, states that:

> Regulated procedures can only be authorised and performed if there are no scientifically suitable alternatives that *replace* animal use, *reduce* the number of animals needed or *refine* the procedures used to cause less suffering – these are known as the 3Rs. In addition, the likely benefits (to humans, other animals or the environment) must be weighed against the likely welfare costs to the animals involved.

All UK scientists are therefore legally obliged to use alternative approaches to the use of animals where possible, to use the minimum number of animals and to use protocols that cause the least pain, suffering or distress. In May 2004 The National Centre for Replacement, Refinement and Reduction of Animals in Research (NC3Rs) was announced. This group is an independent scientific organization tasked by the UK Government with supporting innovation in the bioscience sector by driving the development of new models and tools with reduced reliance on animals and improved animal welfare. The NC3Rs works with research funders, academia, the pharmaceutical and chemical industries and regulatory bodies, both in the UK and internationally, to advance the 3Rs as a framework to address global scientific challenges (see www.nc3rs.org.uk).

Code of conduct

The use of animals in research is also regulated through the ethical codes of individual professional organizations. It is important to distinguish between legislation, which allows transgressions to lead to criminal prosecution, and codes of conduct, which are advisory and at their strongest can only lead to suspension from the professional organization. It is also important to recognize that some animal research is not governed by the Animals Act and therefore the Code of Conduct is important. A Home Office license is only required if a research study could potentially cause pain, suffering, distress or lasting harm to those animals protected by the Act (i.e. vertebrates and octopi).

The British Psychological Society (2007) has produced *Guidelines for Psychologists Working with Animals* The main points of the BPS code in relation to research with non-human animals are:

1 *Legislation.* Psychologists must conform to current legislation.
2 *Replacing the use of animals.* Video records or computer simulations may be useful.
3 *Choice of species.* Should be suited to research purpose and psychologists should be aware of animal's previous experience.
4 *Number of animals.* The smallest number should be used.
5 *Procedures.* Any procedure that may cause pain should be carefully evaluated and alternatives considered. Regulation of food intake (e.g. for conditioning experiments) may be considered to be harmful and researchers should consider an animal's normal food intake and metabolic requirements. Investigators studying animals in the field should minimize interference.
6 *Procurement of animals.* Special guidance is required for wild-caught animals.
7 *Animal care.* Researcher's responsibilities extend to the care of animals when not being studied, including the provision of companions for social animals.
8 *Disposing of animals.* The continuance of a high level of care should be ensured.
9 *Animals in psychology teaching.* Animals may be used but appropriate training should be ensured: for example, individuals might seek a Personal License from the Home Office by attending one of their training courses.
10 *The use of animals for therapeutic purposes,* such as dogs as co-therapists or for use in systematic desensitization. The needs of the animal should be borne in mind so they do not become stressed or tired.
11 *Clinical assessment and treatment of animal behavior.* The Association for the Study of Animal Behavior (ASAB) regulates the therapy given to animals whose behavior is disturbed.

Commentary

Clearly animal research in the UK is carefully regulated both by the law and by a professional code of conduct. However, one problem with codes of conduct is that they remove any need for researchers themselves to think about what they are doing, in terms of right and wrong. Instead researchers may feel no ethical responsibility because it 'has been done for them'. Following the code is sufficient to ensure ethical behavior and therefore researchers may unwittingly behave unethically because they have stopped thinking about what they are doing.

It has also been argued that 'animal' laws may actually legitimize abuse. Dunayer (2002) argues that such laws simply set standards for the imprisonment, enslavement, hurting and killing of animals. Such laws are similar to the laws that codified norms of black enslavement in America; making it legal does not make it right. It can be argued that 'animal' laws should be abolished. They could be replaced with laws that prohibit humans from violating non-human rights. The same laws that protect humans would then protect non-humans, extending rights currently reserved for humans to them all. This sounds very worthy but there is a problem with the idea of animal rights, as we will discuss later in this chapter. In brief, if we extend human rights to cover animals as well, then we would have to grant them other rights too, such as freedom from oppression, a right to paid holiday, a right to nationality and freedom of association (United Nations' Declaration of Human Rights; see Chapter 1). I don't know about you, but the local cat community are not allowed the right of free association in my garden!

A different critical approach is to question whether such laws are effective. PETA (People for the Ethical Treatment of Animals) declares that the American Animal Welfare Act (AWA) 'is very weak and poorly enforced ... It is basically a housekeeping act that does not prohibit any type of animal experimentation' (PETA, 2010). In the UK, the British Union for Abolition of Vivisection (BUAV) has claimed that there are many problems with the Animals Act. In 2007 they took the government to court, arguing that the Act was failing to ensure that numbers of animals in laboratories were being reduced and that animal suffering was being kept to a minimum. However, just before the High Court hearing, the Home Office made certain changes to their practices in order to avert action. Such a response suggests that the law does need policing by activists outside the government.

This need for policing the law is further confirmed by a damning report sponsored by the NC3Rs. Kilkenny et al. (2009) systematically surveyed research reports of studies using animals in the USA and the UK, collecting detailed information from 271 publications. They found that only 59% of reports mentioned the number of animals that were used, that many of the studies reported different numbers of animals in the methods and results sections of the report and that many studies were poorly designed. Kilkenny et al. concluded that there are a number of issues that need to be addressed in animal research: from careful design, as required by the 3Rs, to accurate scientific reporting.

Usefulness: The scientific arguments for using animals in research

At this point we return to the more philosophical debate about the *usefulness* of animals in research: questions about scientific value and ethics. Why use animals at all? The obvious answer to this question is that some research procedures cause harm to participants and therefore would be less acceptable with human participants. This is an ethical issue, which we will return to later. In terms of scientific value, it can be argued that using animals means there are fewer problems with investigator effects (remember that the classic demonstration of investigator effects was in a study using rats by Rosenthal & Fode, 1963 – so there are investigator effects). Animals also breed more rapidly than humans so it is much easier to follow genetic patterns over generations. However, the major justification is that non-human animals and human animals are not so very different, so animal research can tell us a lot about human behavior and physiology.

Generalizing from animal to human behavior

Behaviorists use the theory of evolution to argue that because animals and humans share common ancestors they are composed of the same basic building blocks – behavioral as well as physiological. In humans these building blocks build up to more complex behaviors but, according to behaviorists, the basic units are the same – stimulus–response units that explain conditioning. So, for example, the concept of **learned helplessness** was demonstrated in animals (see Harlow's research earlier in this chapter and Seligman's research in Box 5.3) The principles were applied to the explanation of human depression by Seligman (1975), suggesting that depression is learned when a person tries, but fails, to control unpleasant experiences.

> **KEY TERM**
>
> **Learned helplessness** occurs when an animal finds that its responses are ineffective, and then it learns that there is no point in responding and behaves passively in future.

Commentary

There is no doubt that behaviorist explanations are of considerable relevance to understanding human behavior. Learned helplessness has been extended beyond animal research and demonstrated in humans. For example, Miller and Seligman (1974) found that college students who were exposed to uncontrollable aversive events were subsequently more likely to fail on a similar task.

BOX 5.3   Learned helplessness

Seligman and Maier (1967) placed dogs in a cage where they could not escape from electric shocks being given to their hind legs. Later the same dogs were placed in a different cage where they could escape into a different compartment. In this new environment the dogs did not attempt to move to the safe part of the cage, whereas dogs who had not been exposed to the 'no escape' condition did escape. It was concluded that experience of a situation where escape from aversive stimuli is not possible leads to learning the behavior of helplessness – a passive acceptance of an unpleasant situation.

However, there are many psychologists who would argue that conditioning can never be a complete explanation of *any* behavior. Human behavior is always affected by a host of factors, only some of which influence non-human animals – factors such as social context, emotion and cognitive factors. If such factors do influence animal behavior this would not necessarily result in the same outcomes. In the case of learned helplessness, the model of depression derived from this explanation was later extended to hopelessness theory (Abramson *et al.*, 1989), which explains depression on the basis of pessimistic *expectations* for the future. Thus animal research might provide a useful starting point for understanding human behavior but requires greater complexity in order to provide full explanations.

Generalizing from animal physiology to human physiology

Behaviorists are concerned with human *behavior* (not surprisingly) but another important area of psychological research concerns how our physiology works (i.e. how the body systems work). Human physiology is similar to that of non-human animals in many ways and so, one can argue, it makes sense to conduct invasive procedures on animals in order to make discoveries about human physiology. Examples include the work of Hubel and Wiesel described earlier, in the section on sensory deprivation, demonstrating how the visual cortex works. This work was extended to examine the effects of restricted experience on the development of the visual cortex. If this area of the brain is examined in kittens raised in a vertical striped environment (Blakemore and Cooper's study on p. 102), then it has been found that the cells in the visual cortex that would normally respond to lines of this orientation no longer exist. The brain is altered by experience as long as such experience takes place early in development. Hubel and Wiesel (1970) found that visual deprivation after 8 weeks does not have the same effect.

Such research allows us to make sense of human behavior. Children who are born with a squint (one eye looks in a different direction from the other eye) have difficulty with their binocular vision. Squints can be corrected by performing an operation. However, if this operation is left until after the age of 2 then vision is permanently damaged (Banks et al., 1975). This can be explained in terms of the non-human animal studies. The cells in the visual cortex responsible for making binocular comparisons must have disappeared through lack of experience.

Commentary

There are clearly many physiological comparisons that make sense but others that do not. For example, research on the effects of sleep deprivation (e.g. Jouvet, 1967) and the role of the suprachiasmatic nucleus in the control of biological rhythms (e.g. Morgan, 1995) have both involved stressful procedures with animals (cats and hamsters, respectively). The only justification for such research is what it might tell us about how human biological rhythms function. However, such rhythms may not be controlled in the same way in humans. It might be, for example, that other organs are involved in human biological rhythms.

On the other hand, Green (1994) claims that the basic physiology of the brain and nervous systems of all mammals is essentially the same. Although the human brain might be more highly developed, its similarity to the brains of mammals is far greater than critics of this approach would have us believe.

Comparative studies of the brains and behavior of different animals have been useful also in highlighting the unique features of different species and thus in providing explanations for the differences between the species. For example, the existence of dedicated language areas of the human brain explains the uniqueness of human language.

Alternatives to using animals

In the last few decades a number of new methods have offered alternatives to using animals in research. Computer simulations and brain scanning (Figure 5.6) offer non-invasive methods of studying behavior and physiology. However, some of the same criticisms levied against animal research are relevant here. For example, just because a computer system produces the same output as a human does not mean that the human system functions in the same way. A very

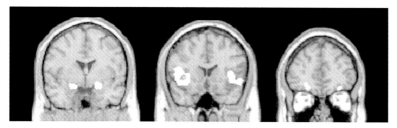

Figure 5.6 Functional magnetic resonance imaging (fMRI) is used to observe the behavior of the brain *in vivo*. Areas of the brain that are rich in oxygen show up on the fMRI scan, indicating the active areas of the brain

simple example of this was the input–output model of the multistore memory model (Atkinson & Shiffrin, 1968), which provided a model for understanding memory. More complex models of memory have been developed but the question remains as to whether such systems can ever reflect the complexity of living organisms.

Drug testing can be done using human tissue cultures. Most recently, possible alternatives for drug testing are being developed in terms of **microdosing**, which means that animals can be exposed to lower risks and human volunteers can be used instead of animals. A review by Rowland (2005) found that microdosing is a promising front-runner in the search to find alternatives for animal testing, although more research is still required to develop the technique. In 2006 EUMAPP (European Union Microdose AMS Partnership Programme) was started to boost Europe's understanding and use of microdosing.

> **KEY TERM**
>
> **Microdosing** Technique for studying the behavior of drugs in humans through the administration of doses so low they are unlikely to produce whole-body effects, but high enough to allow the cellular response to be studied.

The ethical arguments for using animals in research

It is possible that animals are useful in increasing our understanding of human behavior and physiology from a *scientific* viewpoint. But perhaps the main reason to use them is an ethical one – because it is more acceptable to cause harm to a non-human animal than a human. To what extent is this true?

Ethical relativism

In Chapter 1 we looked at absolute and relative morals (see p. 6). This distinction clearly applies to any ethical debate. Ethical relativism is the view that ethical judgements are true or false only relative to a particular context. What might appear unethical here and now, might seem perfectly acceptable in a different environment. You might be a vegetarian with a belief that it is morally wrong (unethical) to eat meat, but if you had the choice of eating meat or dying of starvation then you would probably see your survival as more important than your belief. In the next chapter, we will consider the use of non-human animals in warfare and the work of animal psychologists in modern warfare. The belief that affects your final judgement of the ethics of this work is how necessary you believe the war is. If you were fighting for your survival then you might well think it is acceptable to use animals as agents of war, but if you saw the conflict as a fight over oil supplies, for example, then you would probably see the use of animals as unacceptable. The same points can be applied to your belief in psychological research. The point here is that the judgement of the ethics of using animals is not clear cut and nor can it ever be so. The importance of context is illustrated in Box 5.4. You can see

---

BOX 5.4   When is animal research in psychology acceptable?

Figure 5.7 shows the margin of support that American psychology students expressed for various types of research. Respondents were given an empty table with four columns labeled Primates, Dogs, Rats and Pigeons, and three rows labeled:

Observation

- (observational studies in naturalistic settings).

Confinement

- (research involving caging or confinement, but no physical pain or death).

Pain or death

- (research involving physical pain or death).

They were told to assume that the research was 'institutionally approved and deemed of scientific merit', and they were asked to indicate whether each type of research was usually justified or unjustified. The margin of support equals the percentage of respondents saying justified minus the percentage of respondents saying unjustified (Plous, 1996).

from the graph that context was everything – research with non-human animals was acceptable in observational research, slightly less acceptable when confinement was involved and unacceptable if pain or death was involved.

Assessing pain and suffering

How do we assess pain in an animal that cannot tell us what it is feeling? Sneddon *et al.* (2003) investigated the extent to which fish feel pain. They injected rainbow trout with bee venom and found that they started rocking from side to side, their breathing rate went up and they rubbed their lips on the tank walls. However, we cannot say that the fish *feels pain* just because it responds to the noxious stimulus. The term **sentience** has been used to describe the ability to feel or sense things. This concept is used by Singer in deciding when pain is or is not acceptable, and it is Singer's ideas we turn to next.

KEY TERM

Sentience Being able to sense and feel, and also a subjective awareness of those sensations. For example, sentience is more than just reacting to pain but also a conscious awareness of pain.

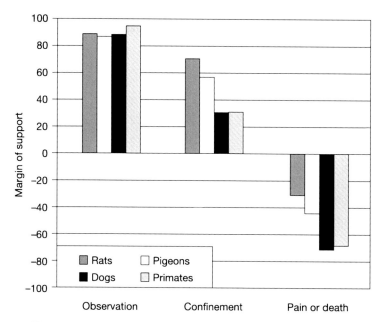

Figure 5.7 Graph showing percentage support for research according to context

Utilitarianism

The utilitarian view is an alternative moral perspective to that of ethical relativism. According to this perspective an action is right or wrong depending upon its consequences. An act is good or moral if it produces the greatest well-being for everyone affected by it. One of the best known supporters of this view in relation to animal research is Peter Singer, a moral philosopher who wrote the classic book *Animal Liberation* in 1975.

The title of the book referred to the fact that animals were being discriminated against in the same way that, in the past, women and blacks had been discriminated against. Singer regarded 'speciesism' as the last remaining form of discrimination that needed to be dealt with by a new liberation movement. Singer argued that the assumption of a superior moral status is wrong, whether it is applied to people from a different ethnic group, women or, in this case, animals. It could be argued that humans are superior to animals because of distinguishing features of humanity, such as high intelligence and complex language. However, this is not true because these characteristics are not present in 'marginal cases' such as young or mentally disabled humans. In addition it has been argued that some supposedly unique human characteristics, such as language, are not unique after all. This means that there is no basis for discriminating between humans and animals and therefore it appears that the only distinction is a prejudice based on species alone.

The utilitarian angle of Singer's argument is that decisions about whether to use animals or not has nothing to do with their worth. If an experiment on a small number of animals can cure disease that affects tens of thousands, it could be justifiable. Singer believes that an individual's well-being or life can be sacrificed to the 'greater good'. This is the basis on which to make ethical decisions about the use of animals.

In fact Singer has extended this argument to clarify the stem cell research debate. He argues that it is sheer species bias that allows us to use sentient non-humans in all sorts of trivial ways, yet some people wish to prevent important research that uses non-sentient human embryos.

KEY TERM

Speciesism A term coined by the psychologist Richard D. Ryder in 1970. It is the assumption that some individuals are superior based solely on the grounds that they are members of the species *Homo Sapiens*. Speciesism is similar to sexism or racism – where superiority is defined by sex or race.

Sentience

Sentience is a key feature of the debate, the point being to distinguish between intellectual capacity (reason) and sensation. The

Compassion in World Farming Trust (CIWF) focuses on the science, policy and cultural implications of animal sentience and comments that 'sentient animals may be aware of a range of sensations and emotions, of feeling pain and suffering, and of experiencing a state of well being' (CIWF, 2010). Psychological research is constantly revealing new capacities in animals that help us to fully understand their sentience (Boyle, 2009).

The issue of sentience goes back a long way; the French philosopher Jean-Jacques Rousseau (1754/1999) argued that the fact that animals are sentient beings 'ought to entitle [animals] at least the privilege of not being wantonly treated by [humans]' (p. 14). In fact now the question of sentience is no longer an issue. In December 2009 the Treaty of Lisbon, which governs the European Union, declared that 'all animals are sentient' (Article III-121) and hence not to be considered as objects or products. At this point it is not clear what the implications will be for the animal debate but it certainly gives Animal Rights campaigners a strong tool in their armoury.

The Animal Rights Movement

Singer's animal liberation view turned into the 'animal *rights* movement', although Singer himself never saw a reason to refer to 'rights'. It can be argued that the concept of rights only arises as part of a contract between members of society. Individuals are given rights in exchange for responsibilities. Animals have no such responsibilities, cannot reciprocate and therefore it does not seem reasonable to say they have rights.

Singer argues that the *interests* of animals should be considered because of their ability to feel suffering and that the idea of rights is not necessary in order to consider that. Nevertheless, you often find the word 'rights' creeping into arguments.

In defense of speciesism

Jeffrey Gray (1991) offered two lines of counter-argument to Singer's view that speciesism is wrong. First he made a distinction between moral and ethical arguments. He agreed that it is *ethically* wrong to inflict pain unnecessarily on any species. However, *moral* choices are different. He uses the example of a mother faced with the choice of having to save two small children from a fire. If one of the children is her own, Gray argues that ethically she should display no preference, but most people would find it morally acceptable that she should choose her own child.

Gray's second counter-argument is developed from this example of the mother and child. It is natural (and thus morally acceptable) for a mother to favor her own child. This makes evolutionary sense (any individual should favor their close relatives above others). The same principle can be extended to favoring one's own species over other species. This is a behavior that is naturally selected. We owe a special duty to our kin and to our own species. As a further example Gray asks what you might do, if you saw two creatures fighting and you have a gun, when: (1) one is your son and the other is a stranger; (2) both are strangers; (3) one is your son and the other is a lion; (4) one is a stranger and the other is a lion. Obviously in situations (1) and (3) people would save their son. In situation (4) Gray claims that most people would shoot the lion because they would regard it morally repugnant to shoot the stranger – the reason is that we have a special duty of care to other human beings just because they are humans.

Singer's reply

Singer (1991) claims that Gray's arguments are flawed in many ways. First, there appears to be no general support for the distinction made between ethics and morals, but, even if we allow this part of Gray's arguments, Singer has more serious objections. The natural selection argument is highly **determinist**, suggesting that human behavior is driven by genetically programed instincts that cannot be overridden by reasoned thought. Gray himself suggested that there are some behaviors that are part of our natural heritage that are not morally acceptable, such as the murder of a sexual rival. This means that it is not sufficient to argue that a behavior is naturally selected and thus acceptable. Furthermore Singer points out that if you open the door to the biological argument there is a lot more that can be 'excused' in human behavior, such as xenophobia and racism.

Finally, Singer agrees that he too would shoot the lion but this does not make him a speciesist. Singer argues that there is a difference between questions of taking life and inflicting pain. It makes sense to save the life of a human but this does not make it acceptable to cause suffering to an animal.

KEY TERM

Determinist The view that an individual's behavior is shaped or controlled by internal or external forces rather than an individual's will to do something.

REFLECTIVE EXERCISE 5.4

Singer argues that there is a difference between questions of taking life and inflicting pain. Try devising a similar test to the one used by Gray, which would assess people's preferences about harming animals versus humans in various circumstances.

Use your test to find out people's reactions.

The psychologist Richard Wiseman (2010) tried one where he said:

> Imagine walking into a room and finding your beloved dog or cat, and a randomly selected two year old child that you have never seen before. You are presented with a simple choice. You have to press one of three buttons. One button will instantly kill your pet. The second button will instantly kill the child and the third button will instantly kill you.

Which button would you select?

The absolutist position – empty cages

Singer's utilitarian approach is a relativist position; there are those who take an absolutist stance. For example, Tom Regan (1984) takes the view that some animal species should never be used in research no matter what the benefits and no matter how well their needs are looked after. In his book *Empty Cages* Regan (2004) suggests that justice does not demand larger, cleaner cages for animal subjects but empty cages. He argues that human ethics is based on the independent value of the individual and to ignore this individual value, even applied to animals, is to violate that most basic of human rights: the right of each individual to be treated with respect.

Central to Regan's philosophy is the concept 'subject of a life'. He claims that any individual who is the 'subject of a life' has inherent value to that individual that is independent of any usefulness to others. Any individual (human or animal) who has inherent value has a right to be treated with respect and a right not to be used. It should be noted that Regan believes that all mature mammals are 'subject of a life' but it is not clear to what extent this applies to other animals. This means that *no* mature mammals should be treated any differently from humans.

KEY TERM

Subject of a life A way to describe the fact that some animals are more than merely alive and conscious. Subjects-of-a-life are characterized by a set of features including having beliefs, feelings, memory and self-awareness.

In a sense Regan's approach has been supported by legislation, which bans the use of chimpanzees, gorillas and orang-utans in research.

Conclusion

Attitudes towards the use of animals have changed enormously over the last 50 years. Singer (2003) notes that prior to 1970 only 94 works had ever been published on the moral status of animals, whereas between 1970 and 1988 more than double that number were published.

Reasoned argument and legislation are continuing to produce more humane and thoughtful ways of dealing with animals. The pledge by the UK government to refine, reduce and replace animals in research offers a viable future strategy for balancing costs and benefits. However, it seems clear that efforts to do this must remain closely monitored.

Summary

Animals have been used in psychological studies in a number of ways, most of which raise serious concerns about the harm done to animal subjects. Legislation and codes of practice offer some controls over animal research, although it has not been 100% effective. The concept of the 3Rs (*refine, replace, reduce*) is intended to guide future decisions about what is permissible. The usefulness of animals relates to ethics (animals are preferable to humans) and scientific value (animals are similar to humans). In terms of scientific value, animal research may provide some insights into human behavior and physiology but recent technological developments offer useful alternatives, such as brain scans and microdosing. In terms of ethics, there is a range of arguments — moral relativism, ultilitarianism (Singer) and absolutism (Regan).

FURTHER READING

* Blum, D. (2003) *Love at Goon Park: Harry Harlow and the Science of Affection.* Chichester: Wiley. [Lengthy descriptions of Harlow's research, and insights into the man himself.]
* Gray, J.A. (1991) On the morality of speciesism. *The Psychologist, 14,* 196–198.
* Kilkenny, C., Parsons, N., Kadyszewski, E., Festing, F.W., Cuthill, I.C., Fry, D., Hutton, J. & Altman, D.G. (2009) survey of the quality of experimental design, statistical analysis and reporting of research using animals. *PLoS ONE, 4(11).* [Can be accessed at www.plosone.org/article/info:doi/10.1371/journal.pone.0007824]
* Singer, P. (1975) *Animal Liberation.* New York: Avon. [A revised and updated version was published in 2009 by Harper Perennial.]
* Singer, P. (1991) Speciesism, morality and biology: A response to Jeffrey Gray. *The Psychologist, 14,* 199–200.
* Singer, P. (2003) Animal liberation at 30. *The New York Review of Books, 50(8).* [Singer reviews the Animal Rights Movement 30 years after the publication of his book.]

WEBSITES

* Animals (Scientific procedures) Act
  http://www.archive.official-documents.co.uk/document/hoc/321/321-xa.htm
* BPS guidelines for using animals
  www.bps.org.uk/document-download-area/document-download.cfm?file_uuid=DA9509C9-1143-DFD0-7EE7-9D998D01F023&ext=pdf
* Dian Fossey gorilla site
  www.gorillafund.org/

Organizations supporting animal research
* Understanding animal research
  www.understandinganimalresearch.org.uk/
* National Centre for Replacement, Refinement and Reduction of Animals in Research
  www.nc3rs.org.uk
* Psychologists for the ethical treatment of animals
  www.psyeta.org/

Organizations against animal research
* British Union for the Abolition of Vivisection
  www.buav.org/
* People for the Ethical Treatment of Animals
  www.peta.org
* Washoe
  www.friendsofwashoe.org/

Psychology in practice 6

What this chapter will teach you

- Ethics are easier to resolve on paper than in real life
- The special ethical dilemmas created by military action
- The media has an ethical code all of its own
- The rights of mental health patients are sometimes in conflict with the behavior of psychologists

This chapter looks at some of the ethical dilemmas that arise with the practice of psychology. We have chosen our examples to give you a flavor of the work that psychologists do and the dilemmas they encounter. We start with military psychology, and move on to how psychologists conduct themselves in the media, how they behave towards their clients and how they choose to speak out or stay silent about important issues. The health warning that goes with this chapter says that we have chosen a number of controversial examples to make our points and we hope you do not end up with the impression that all psychologists are scurrilous disreputable charlatans.

Military psychology

The ethics of warfare are difficult to unravel. If you are a pacifist and would never use violence and believe we should not use weapons against other human beings, then the moral issue is clear – fighting is wrong. Many people, however, are prepared to fight or even use weapons in certain circumstances, for example to protect themselves, their family and friends or even their property. They might be prepared to fight for a cause and they might believe that some military acts are morally justified. Some people might not want to fight but will be prepared to allow someone else to fight on their behalf. Whatever you believe, it is clear that armies and warfare have been a major influence on the development of human societies and continue to be so. Thousands of men and women in this country and abroad are employed by military forces and millions are affected by military actions.

Psychology has been involved with the military for 100 years and its involvement raises a number of ethical issues. The most fundamental of these is whether you believe it is right to help a military organization become more efficient. If you are a pacifist then the answer is obviously 'no', but if you accept the need for an army then it makes sense to use all the resources at your disposal, including psychologists.

REFLECTIVE EXERCISE 6.1

1 Under what conditions would you think it is right to be aggressive to another person or group of people? Is it ever morally justified to go to war? And if not, what steps do you think should be taken to stop your country from going to war?
2 If someone has information that would be useful in saving the lives of other people, how far would you go to get that information?

The American Psychological Association (APA) has a division of military psychology. This division encourages research and the application of psychological research to military problems. It is well respected and the research attracts a lot of funding, so what do they do?

Up until the 1960s, military psychology was mainly concerned with the same issues that would concern any major employer of people;

- selection of appropriate staff
- matching people (soldiers) to machines
- training (military) specialists
- staff welfare.

An article in *American Psychologist* by Windle and Vallance (1964) reflected the change that began to take place in military psychology in the 1960s. The article suggested that psychology was turning its attention to paramilitary issues, for example studies to investigate the political motivations of guerrilla fighters, the human factors in underground organizations, and so on. Some of the other issues that this new type of psychology investigated were:

- the effects of captivity
- interrogation techniques
- brain-washing.

Today military psychologists look at a range of issues, including the psychology of military organization, the psychology of military life and the psychology of combat. To be truthful, much of the research is classified as secret so we do not have a complete picture of what is being studied. Before we develop too many conspiracy theories, however, let us have a look at some classic pieces of military psychology that raise some ethical issues.

Animals at war

Animals have been trained using behavioral techniques to become agents of human warfare. Most recently, in the Iraq War in 2003, sea lions were used to put handcuffs on enemy divers (*Daily Mail*, 2009). In the past an ark-full of animals have been enlisted, including cats, dogs, seagulls, dolphins and pigeons. Most famously B.F. Skinner showed that it was possible to use pigeons as a guidance system in a missile. To cut a long, though interesting, story short, Skinner (1960) showed that his pigeons could accurately pilot a missile to seek out ships, and then could discriminate between different types of ships so that they could fly past allied ships and dive onto enemy ships. The military got as far as modifying some of their missiles to accommodate the pigeons and their tracking apparatus. However, the pigeons were never brought into active service.

Many readers might be appalled at the callous disregard for the pigeons. If the project had been brought into operation, Skinner would have trained pigeons that would then unwittingly be the agents of their own destruction as they guided themselves, and their missiles, towards detonation on an enemy ship. Ethics, however, must always be seen in the context of the times. During the Second World War it appeared to many people that it was right to go to war against Nazism, and that this war should be concluded as soon as possible to avoid defeat and further loss of life. In his paper Skinner writes: 'The ethical question of our right to convert a lower creature into an unwitting hero is a peace-time luxury' (Skinner, 1960, p. 28). You might still not accept this as a justification for the use of animals in warfare, but it does highlight that the issue of ethics is not a simple one and that people sometimes choose to act by criteria that conflict with their normal moral standards.

REFLECTIVE EXERCISE 6.2

Look back at Chapter 5 on the ethics of using animals in research. Are there any other ethics that you would add for the training of animals by psychologists for use in warfare?

If we look back at the categories of ethical judgements first described in Chapter 1, then we might argue that the *consequences* of using animals in warfare (i.e. reducing the number of human deaths and injuries) provide an adequate justification.

Sensory deprivation

One of the most controversial contributions of psychology has been the development of **sensory deprivation** (SD) techniques. Donald Hebb was a leading figure in Canadian psychology and received substantial funding from the military to investigate this phenomenon (McCoy, 2007). The question that they studied concerned the response people have to being removed from the common sensations of everyday life. What happens if you are in a place with no obvious changes in sight, sound or temperature, and with nothing to do?

KEY TERM

Sensory deprivation The cutting out of all incoming sensory information, or at least as much of it as possible. Sometimes used as a method of torture.

Volunteer students were kept in isolation in an air-conditioned room. They wore translucent goggles so that they could only see a blur of light. The only sound they heard was a constant buzzing noise and they had to wear long cuffs so that they could not touch anything. As an incentive they were offered $20 for every day they could stay in the room (about a week's wages in today's money), and they each had a 'panic button' that they could press to obtain instant release. They were provided with a comfortable bed and decent food (Hebb *et al.*, 1952).

To start with the volunteers tended to sleep, but soon they found that it became increasingly difficult to concentrate and they developed an acute desire for any kind of stimulation to break the monotony. Many started to experience startling visual and auditory hallucinations, and after a while they were unable to distinguish waking from sleeping. Despite the high pay for just lying on their backs, only a few lasted more than 2 days and the most anyone lasted was 5 days. When released they were given simple psychological tests, which showed that their perceptions had become very disorientated, with objects appearing blurred and fuzzy. More important from the investigators' point of view, while under the SD conditions they were found to be much more susceptible to *any* type of propaganda.

There have been many more studies on this, including immersing people in lukewarm water to further reduce the stimulation (Lilly, 1956), or just leaving people alone in a silent room (Smith & Lewty, 1959). In all the studies it does not take long for the participants to have severe psychological reactions, including disordered thinking, loss of identification, panic, body-image distortions and violent nightmares (Zubek, 1969).

A variation on the SD technique was used by the British Army in Northern Ireland in the early days of 'The Troubles'. Shallice (1972) reported on 12 internees who were subjected to a horrifying interrogation technique. In the gaps between direct interrogation, the men were hooded in a black woven bag, subjected to very loud white noise and forced to stand against a wall with their hands above their heads. They were required to stand there for up to 16 hours and if they moved they were beaten. The internees were required to wear loose boiler suits, were sleep deprived and put on a restricted diet. This treatment had a devastating effect on the men, who had major physical, cognitive and emotional responses (McGuffin, 1974).

The military interest in the SD studies is twofold: how to prepare their own troops for the rigors of captivity, and how to encourage prisoners to talk. It is this second issue that raises the ethical issues. From an absolutist point of view, it is wrong to subject people to psychological torture, but what if that person has information that might save the lives of thousands? Would you still give them a cup of tea and a biscuit? Nothing is easy in this moral maze.

Guantanamo Bay

This discussion of sensory deprivation brings us to Guantanamo Bay on the coast of Cuba. In 2002 the USA set up a prison camp outside of its home territory, and therefore outside US law, to house the people it was capturing around the world who they believed were terrorists. The President at the time, George W. Bush, said that these people were not soldiers and hence not subject to the protection offered by the Geneva Convention. In some cases the people were taken from conflict zones in Afghanistan and Pakistan, and in some cases they were snatched from countries where there was no conflict. Some were taken through UK facilities on their way to Guantanamo.

To describe the full horror of Guantanamo would take a book in itself, and if you want to know more about it then just search the internet. The issue we want to look at in this book is the role of psychologists at Guantanamo and also at other modern military prisons. The role of Guantanamo was not just to contain these people but to get information from them about possible attacks on Western countries, and so interrogation techniques were very important. This is where psychologists come in and one of the many techniques they were able to bring along was sensory deprivation. If you look at the image in Figure 6.1 you will see prisoners at Guantanamo in orange jump suits.

Figure 6.1 Sensory deprivation used on prisoners at the US Guantanamo torture camp

If you look closer you will see that they have ear muffs (so they cannot hear anything), opaque glasses (so they cannot see anything) and thick gloves (so they cannot feel anything). This is sensory deprivation. And they have shackles on their ankles and wrists, which is why they appear to be praying.

The involvement of psychologists in military interrogation has created a storm through the profession. In most people's eyes, the interrogation of people who are being held outside international law (i.e. illegally) is unethical in itself, but to then subject them to inhumane treatment can be classed as torture, and to continue with this over a period of years is beyond description. There does not appear to be an ethical dilemma here because it is clearly wrong, or is it?

The use of health professionals, including psychologists, in abusive interrogation techniques is now well documented (e.g. Soldz, 2007). The interrogations at Guantanamo were overseen by a Behavioral Science Consultation Team (BSCT) that included psychologists (Lifton, 2004), and the team prepared psychological profiles for the interrogators to use. It is also clear that 'since late 2002 ... psychologists have been part of a strategy that employs extreme stress, combined with behavior shaping rewards, to extract actionable intelligence from resistant captives' (Bloche & Marks, 2005, p. 6).

At the same time as Guantanamo was operating, the USA were taking charge of a military prison in Baghdad during the invasion of Iraq. The military brought to the Abu Ghraib prison the techniques they had developed at Guantanamo (Soldz, 2007) and psychologists were at the forefront of this operation. This prison hit the news when pictures of the degrading treatment being inflicted on the inmates were sent to a newspaper. Some junior soldiers were tried and imprisoned for this but their commanders were not. In interviews the guards described how they were responding to what they perceived to be the requests of PsyOps (Psychological Operations) unit. One of those charged, Private Lynndie England, who featured prominently in the first batch of photographs and was subsequently jailed, insisted she was acting on orders from 'persons in my chain of command': 'I was instructed by persons in higher rank to "stand there, hold this leash, look at the camera", and they took pictures for PsyOps' (see, for example, Ronson, 2005).

The ethics of interrogation

In 2002, just as Guantanamo was coming on line, the APA made a change in its ethical code. This change concerned situations where a psychologist comes into conflict between the orders they are being given and their ethical code. So, for example, if they were a member of the military and were asked to carry out an inhumane interrogation that is against the ethical code of psychologists, what should they do? Should they go with their ethical code or should they follow their orders? This is an easy decision when sat in a comfy chair reading a book but a much harder one in a real-life situation.

The response of the APA could have been to put pressure on the military and the US Government not to carry out torture and not to require psychologists to be part of it. What they did, however, was to change their ethical code to give psychologists a get-out clause to take part in the torture. The new code said: 'If the conflict is un-resolvable [between orders and ethics] psychologists may adhere to the requirements of the law, regulations, or other governing legal authority' (APA, 2002a).

This addition to the APA ethics code hit a nerve in the USA and the UK because it is an echo of the Nuremberg Defence. This is the moral defense for war crimes that says 'it wasn't my fault, I was obeying orders'. It is called the **Nuremberg Defense** because it was used by the people who were put on trial for war crimes after the Second World War (1939–1945). The defense was rejected at those trials, so it made it all the more controversial to add this defense to the APA ethical code.

The APA was put under intense pressure over its stance and eventually sent a delegation to look at the Guantanamo facility led by the then president Ronald Levant, who wrote:

> I accepted this invitation to visit Guantanamo because I saw it as an important opportunity for the Association to provide input on the question of how psychologists can play an appropriate and ethical role in national security investigations.
>
> (Levant, 2007, p. 2)

He was accompanied on the trip by Steven Sharfstein, President of the American Psychiatric Association, who was so alarmed by what he encountered that he called for all psychiatrists to have nothing more to do with military interrogations. No such clear statement came from the APA and the involvement of psychologists continued at military interrogation facilities.

Most revealing in Levant's description of what he encountered at Guantanamo is the following:

> We next visited the brand new psychiatric wing, which has both inpatient and outpatient services. I had a very unusual experience as we were standing at the nursing station, receiving a briefing from the psychiatrist. Behind me a voice asked 'Dean Levant? Is that you?' That was the last thing I expected to hear at GTMO! I turned to see a former doctoral student in clinical psychology from Nova Southeastern University (NSU), who is now a military psychologist. I thought to myself, 'NSU's graduates sure have done a good job of getting out into the world!'
>
> (Levant, 2007, p. 5)

Study psychology, see the world and use sensory deprivation techniques on kidnap victims. It is a catchy slogan, but it might not attract the business that psychology wants.

The APA was always clear in its opposition to the use of torture but less clear in what to do when faced with the moral conflict of being ordered to behave outside its professional ethical code. When the APA tried to deal with this ethical issue it turned to a task force of ten experts. Remarkably, it is reported that six of these experts had military training and at least four of whom had worked at Guantanamo Bay or Abu Ghraib – the military prison in Iraq (Soldz, 2007). Finally, in 2009 there was a change in government of the USA and President Obama brought in a new attitude to Guantanamo and clearly stated that he did not want Americans involved in torture. The APA also changed its line and amended its ethical code as follows:

> REFLECTIVE EXERCISE 6.3
>
> What are the differences between interrogation and torture? Is torture ever justified?

> The APA Ethics Committee will not accept any defense to torture in its adjudication of ethics complaints.
>
> Torture in any form, at any time, in any place, and for any reason, is unethical for psychologists and wholly inconsistent with membership in the American Psychological Association.
>
> (APA, 2009)

This all sounds like a very negative story about psychology and psychologists and it is obviously not the profession's finest hour. However, during the time that Guantanamo was operational many psychologists kept up a barrage of articles that challenged the APA's position and some decided to leave the APA (e.g. Pope & Gutheil, 2009). The debate about ethics was kept going throughout this time and eventually the APA arrived at a result that was in agreement with other similar professions, such as doctors and psychiatrists.

Ethical issues in military psychology

Psychology has been used as a weapon of war across the world. The examples we have looked at concern the actions of the US military. This is not because the Americans are the only people to use these tactics, nor are they by any stretch of the imagination the worst, but they are the most reported and recorded army anywhere and so the information is readily available.

So what are the ethical issues about military psychology? We have raised the negatives in the above examples, but it is possible to argue a positive case for the use of psychology in the military. We might argue that the use of psychology can reduce injury or the loss of life. Anything that speeds up a conflict will bring nearer the time of peace. We might also argue that some conflicts are morally justified and therefore it is appropriate to use psychology to advance the cause. It is also worth pointing out that much of the work of military psychologists is in the management of service personnel and their care and protection. Psychology has a lot to say about the response of combatants and civilians to warfare and can make some valuable contributions (Summerfield, 2000).

> ### REFLECTIVE EXERCISE 6.4
>
> Make a list of what psychology can be used for in warfare and consider when these activities might be justified. You can think about how psychology might help the armed forces to do their job more effectively, how it might help to keep the public supporting the war or how it might be used against other groups to destabilize and demoralize them.

The easier ethical issue concerns the decision to take part or not. The more complicated issues arise after you have decided on that one. Psychologists who decide to take part in military activity still have to draw lines. It is also fair to say that those of us who decide not to take part still enjoy the benefits of living in a successful and militarily powerful society, so we cannot just wash our hands of it and protest our innocence.

Media psychologists

The behavior of professional psychologists raises a number of ethical issues. They have personal interactions with clients that are guided by a code of conduct, they make contributions to the media and they develop theories and techniques that have a direct effect on the public (see also the section in Chapter 3 on talking to the media).

Psychologists have become increasingly involved with the media over the last 20 years, commonly offering advice on personal problems and comments on behavior and events (Canter & Breakwell, 1986). Newspaper advice columns, magazine self-improvement articles, psychology books, radio phone-in shows, talk show appearances, experts on the TV news and consultants for films and TV shows are among the many opportunities for psychologists to be in the media (Bouhoutsos et al., 1986).

Raviv et al. (1989) noted that the window of opportunity opened for psychomedia with the revision to the American Psychiatric Association Code of Ethics in 1981, permitting 'personal advice' but not 'therapy' on the air. The ambiguity between personal advice and therapy led to, and continues to create, a lot of controversy but also gave the green light to a new genre of media psychology.

Because psychologists are looked upon as experts in the field of human relations, they are also often interviewed by journalists to shed light on a particular issue, incident or area of interest (Frank, 1983). This can become a problem as, in the media, information is often presented in a superficial way due to time demands, or space limitations, and thus a psychologist's statements may be misinterpreted or presented inaccurately. We need to develop a new ethical code to deal with these interactions and Box 6.1 shows some suggestions offered by Keith-Spiegel and Koocher (1985). The suggestions are incorporated in the APA ethical guidelines and you can see these in full on their website

BOX 6.1 Suggestions for psychologists dealing with the media by Keith-Spiegel and Koocher (1985)

1 Find out the purpose of the story; if it sounds exploitive, consider waiting for another opportunity to make your material public.

2 Give the reporter a written statement, if possible, to reduce the chance of misquotes.

3 Invite the reporter to call you back if questions arise, or for an editorial review.

4 Refuse comment on an area where you have insufficient knowledge, and, if possible, make a referral to an informed source.

5 Call back if you believe you made an error.

6 Qualify all salient or dramatic remarks, and avoid making offhand comments.

7 Do not speak for the profession as a whole.

8 Admit when you do not have an answer, rather than formulating an ill-informed one.

9 If the topic is controversial, suggest that the reporter contact other colleagues as well.

10 Offer only possibilities when asked to comment on situations for which no solid data exist (e.g. a hostage situation).

11 Psychological evaluations about newsworthy individuals should be avoided and confidentiality should be observed at all times.

12 If you are dissatisfied about the final product, let the reporter know in a constructive way.

(see end of chapter for link). It is fair to say that many psychologists are very careful about their dealings with the media but this is a text about ethical issues so we will look at some examples of psychologists' work that raise some concerns.

Inside the mind of Paul Gascoigne

On 10 July 2003, Channel 4 showed a film entitled *Inside the Mind of Paul Gascoigne*. Gascoigne (Gazza) was a professional footballer (oh you must have heard of him) of exceptional talent who has attracted massive media attention for most of his adult life. This program set out to show that he is in some mental distress and to provide as many labels as possible for that distress. As *The Guardian* wrote the next day: 'Where would TV be without experts?' The program used experts, including psychologist Professor Kevin Gournay, to suggest that Gascoigne is suffering from three varieties of mental disorder: attention deficit disorder, obsessive–compulsive disorder and Tourette's syndrome. The diagnosis was reached without a personal examination of Gascoigne but as *The Guardian*'s TV reviewer wrote: 'Professor Kevin Gournay seemed pretty convinced'. Once Gournay had provided the academic gloss to this program, Gascoigne's friends and colleagues queued up to report how 'mad' he is. Subsequent press reports now commonly describe Gascoigne with the diagnostic labels used in the program. On the Channel 4 website it says:

> According to psychologists, Paul's manic energy, short attention span and childish, inappropriate behavior are all symptoms of a mental condition known as Attention Deficit Disorder (ADD). Paul also appears to suffer from Obsessive Compulsive Disorder (OCD), an illness where overwhelming anxiety is relieved by repetitive behavior, such as obsessive tidying or over-exercising.
>
> Paul admits to such obsessive behaviors, but puts them down to stress; they were his way of handing a situation that he wasn't happy with. Furthermore, his well-documented twitches, grimaces and outbursts are classic symptoms of a neurological disorder that often accompanies OCD – Tourette Syndrome.
>
> (http://www.channel4.com/health/microsites/P/paul_gascoigne/index.html)

Let us unpick the ethics of this. If Gascoigne was a patient of Gournay, then the therapist would not be at liberty to discuss him for reasons of confidentiality. Gournay can only discuss him because he does not know him, but what are the professional ethics of commenting on someone you have never met and publicly attaching damaging psychiatric labels to them? Gascoigne disputes the diagnosis (given above) but his point of view is not given the same weight as that of the absent expert. Furthermore, if Gascoigne does indeed have some serious mental health problems, then how is his welfare helped by Gournay's contribution? Has he not further added to the distress of the man and thereby amplified whatever problems he had? And is there not an alternative explanation for Gascoigne's behavior in his victimization by the media for many years? Gournay might well have commented on the psychological pressure of not even being able to have a pizza without someone taking a photograph of you, although that might not have fitted the agenda of the program and he would not have got so much air time. Professor Gournay is a very wise man, and very wise men make a point of saying what people want to hear.

The Big Brother psychologists

The *Big Brother* programs are a (Western) worldwide phenomenon. A group of young people are put in a house and observed 24 hours a day. They are given strict rules of behavior so they cannot challenge the nature of the show or define their own lives. They are effectively human goldfish. One of the regular features is for psychologists to comment on their behavior and their relationships. Below is an example of these comments as reported on the *Big Brother* website:

> A *Big Brother* psychologist has been studying the housemates' different reactions to newcomer X. His attention, in these early stages in particular, is focused on Y. From the first introductions, the psychology team noticed behavioral traits that separated Y from the rest of the group. 'Y's posture was very closed towards X' said the psychologist. 'The others as a group were very open.'
>
> Even Y's smile came under scrutiny. 'It was a strange smile that abruptly changed to a neutral expression, hinting that it was never a genuine smile at all. X is a threat to Y. So far, Y has had most of the boys running after her. What we can expect to see now is Y being more pro-active with her flirting. She has competition and will have to put in more effort.'
>
> (*Big Brother*, 2000)

What are the ethical issues in this you may ask? Is it not just harmless entertainment? As ever, it depends on your view of what is happening. We would argue that it misrepresents psychology and is potentially damaging to the contestants. On the first point, we have to be clear that psychologists *cannot* read minds, *cannot* read intentions, *cannot* read body language, *cannot* read palms and *cannot* see into the future. They cannot tell everything about you from looking at your 'body language', and, while we are at it, they cannot 'read' tea leaves or handwriting. A training in psychology will not give you these skills.

David Wilson was the *Big Brother* psychologist in 2004 and resigned because of the harm he believed the production company (Endemol) were intentionally doing. He advised them that to readmit some ejected housemates to the house after they had been able to listen to what the other housemates had said about them would be a recipe for disaster. They went ahead and Wilson resigned (Wilson, 2005). Wilson questions why the other psychologists employed by Endemol have been prepared to sit by while housemates have been humiliated and distressed by their experiences in the house. The ethics of media involvement are difficult to call but you would hope that psychologists would look to defend people's well-being and dignity.

Britney Spears and Dr. Phil

Britney Spears is a US singer/songwriter who has sold tens of millions of albums worldwide over the last 10 years. She has been the subject of intense media interest and since 2007 some of that interest has focused on her perceived mental health. She has had some problems and been admitted to psychiatric facilities, and there has been public speculation about what, if any, diagnosis she has been given.

Phillip McGraw is best known as Dr. Phil, an American TV celebrity with a therapy show plus numerous other media ventures. In January 2008 McGraw visited Britney Spears in her hospital room in Los Angeles, California. There is some confusion about whether he was invited to visit, but if he was it was not by Britney Spears. When he left the hospital McGraw issued a statement to the media in which he said:

> My meeting with Britney and some of her family members this morning in her room at Cedars leaves me convinced more than ever that she is in dire need of both medical and psychological intervention. I am very concerned for her.
>
> (*New York Daily News*, 2008)

Let us put aside for one minute whether he has a license to practice psychology in California (he does not have one in Texas) and just look at the ethics of this statement. If you have been invited to counsel a distressed person it is clear that you cannot immediately report to the media on their mental condition. Even if you are hoping to do a 'TV special' on that person in your next show, you cannot do that.

Dr. Phil is an extreme case of a media personality who makes a substantial income from his various commercial interests that are commonly described as psychology. Media personalities such as Dr. Phil are an important part of the image that people have of psychology.

The upside of psychology on the media is that it can bring psychological ideas to the general public – it can inform and educate. However, it can also trivialize, misrepresent and do a lot of harm to individuals and also might put people off from seeking help for their psychological troubles.

> ## REFLECTIVE EXERCISE 6.5
>
> Have a look at the ethical principles described earlier in this book and see which ones you think Dr. Phil has broken with his intervention with Britney Spears.

Psychologists and therapy

One of the most prominent areas of professional psychology is concerned with the support of people with mental or behavioral disorders. This contact with distressed and vulnerable people provides psychologists with great opportunities to contribute positively to our society but also raises some socially sensitive ethical issues.

Manufacturing victims

Professional workers need clients or they are out of a job. Doctors need patients, the police need criminals, soldiers need conflict and psychologists need the business. Mental distress is big business and psychologists have a part to play in that business. One part is to provide support and help to people who are in distress, but not everyone believes it stops there. Dineen (1999) is a critic of the therapy industry (as she calls it) and, according to her, most psychologists do more harm than good and are actively engaged in the business of turning as many of us as possible into 'victims' prepared to pay for therapy.

Although much of her argument focuses on entrepreneurial psychology in North America, what she has to say is relevant to any society in which faith is placed in counselors, therapists, traumatologists and anyone else who happens to thinks they can explain all our current ills, from minor anxieties to crime and economic failure, in pseudo-psychological terms. What she objects to, in short, is quackery and in her book (*Manufacturing Victims: What the Psychology Industry Is Doing to People*) she describes many examples of it.

In some ways, of course, psychology is a soft target. The misuse of **Recovered Memory Therapy**, where patients allegedly recover buried memories of sexual or satanic abuse (often with dramatic legal consequences), is easy to criticize (see the section on the work of Elizabeth Loftus in Chapter 4, p. 91). Absurdities like 'llama therapy' (where llamas are used to teach young offenders to feel empathy) and therapists offering treatment for people feeling 'enslaved by email' are even easier to deride. Dineen, however, is not simply concerned about things that are obviously scandalous or absurd. She is concerned about the whole scientific foundation of the discipline. A large part of her book focuses on examples of fraudulent research and on the failure of psychologists to show that their various therapies benefit anyone other than themselves.

> **KEY TERM**
>
> **Recovered Memory Therapy** A term used by to describe a range of psychiatric techniques based on recalling memories of childhood experiences that had been forgotten. The techniques are very controversial because the balance of evidence is that unpleasant experiences can not be completely repressed and forgotten, and false memories can be easily created during therapy.

Consider this: After a newsworthy horrific event such as the mass killing in Whitehaven in the summer of 2010, you hear on the news that a team of psychologists has been sent to the area to deal with the initial reaction – why? Is there any evidence that an immediate intervention by psychologists or therapists has any beneficial effect? Surely grief is as old as humanity itself and dealing with grief is something that people have had to do since they first realized what death means. On the whole, people do not want psychologists turning up to see if they are alright. For example, a study of responses to the London bombs of 2005 found that only 1% thought they needed professional help to deal with their reaction (Rubin *et al.*, 2005). One of the authors, Simon Wessely from the Institute of Psychiatry, argued:

> Post-traumatic counselling is a bad idea and a bad intervention … it assumes normal people are too incompetent to deal with adversity and it takes attention and resources away from those people who really do need help from interventions that work.
>
> (BPS, 2006, p. 518)

A meta-analysis (which puts together the data from several studies to get a bigger picture) found that there is no evidence that single-session individual psychological debriefing is a useful treatment for the prevention of post-traumatic stress disorder (PTSD) after traumatic incidents. Single debriefing does not prevent the onset of PTSD nor reduce psychological distress, compared to control groups. Also there is no evidence of medium- or long-term benefits of the counseling (Rose et al., 2009). Given this evidence, the ethical approach would be to stop sending teams of psychologists to every disaster scene. Don't hold your breath though, because there are other issues that come into play, such as the need for the authorities to do something and be seen to be doing something, regardless of whether it is any use.

KEY TERMS

Post-traumatic stress disorder An anxiety disorder resulting from experience with a catastrophic event beyond the normal range of human suffering, and characterized by numbness to the world, reliving the trauma in dreams and memories and symptoms of anxiety.

Diagnostic and Statistical Manual of Mental Disorders The categorization and description of mental disorders. It is published by the American Psychiatric Association and is widely used in the USA and to varying degrees around the world by diagnosticians and policy makers.

Diagnostic and Statistical Manual of Mental Disorders (DSM)

One of the significant contributions of psychologists and psychiatrists to the treatment of mental disorders in the USA is the *Diagnostic and Statistical Manual of Mental Disorders* (DSM). The current version runs to 900 pages and describes more than 300 mental disorders. The DSM is used to classify mental disorders and to give them a diagnosis. The DSM is an American invention but it is becoming increasingly used in the UK. The widely used international alternative is the World Health Organization's ICD (*International Statistical Classification of Diseases and Related Health Problems*) (see http://www.who.int/whosis/icd10/).

The DSM structures the way we think about life, behavior and experience and defines many sorts of behavior as mental disorders, some of which do not seem to deserve the label of mental disorder. For example, it has a disorder called *oppositional defiant disorder*, something you or I might well call 'being awkward', and another disorder called *conduct disorder*, which might be called 'naughtiness' by someone else.

The danger of the DSM is that it can turn everyday behavior into pathological categories, thereby creating work for psychologists, among others, and assigning negative labels to ordinary people. In case you think we are exaggerating the problem, you might consider an article in a prestigious journal that reports that a third of us have 'excessive anxiety' when asked to speak to large audiences and may be suffering from a mental disorder (Stein *et al.*, 1996). It seems entirely reasonable, to the authors, to be very anxious about speaking in public and especially so to a big audience, and it is difficult to see this anxiety as a sign of mental disorder. The story of the DSM, its rise to dominance and the different interest groups that influence its development are described excellently by Kutchins and Kirk (2002) if you would like to check this out.

The DSM raises ethical issues because of the behaviors it decides to classify as a disorder and because of the uses to which it is put. With regard to the first point, there have been long and bitter debates over the years about how to classify homosexual behavior and how to classify the behavior of the women in abusive relationships. The way you classify these behaviors will affect how people are seen and are dealt with, so it is not just a theoretical exercise. With regard to the uses of the DSM, it must be said that a diagnosis can be worth a lot of money. It can be worth money to the patient because if you want to sue an employer for causing your illness you have to have a diagnosis. It can also be worth a lot of money to the pharmaceutical industry because for every diagnosis there is a medication you can use. You might not be surprised to read that some of the main funders of DSM development are the pharmaceutical companies. The world thinks it is going mad because the drug companies tell it so, and psychologists collude in this nonsense because it is good for our business as well.

To give you an idea of the scale of the issue, have a look at the figures for psychiatric medication for one disorder in England. In 2003, doctors made out 27,700,000 prescriptions for antidepressants (Department of Health, 2004), which is an awful lot of pills and a figure that would raise a few eyebrows. However, the latest data show that in 2008 in England there were 37,000,000 prescriptions for antidepressants (Health and Social Care Information Centre, 2009) at a cost of over £250 million, which is an increase of 33% in only 5 years.

It is hard to justify this level of medication, especially given the growing body of research suggesting antidepressants have about the same effect as placebos for all but the most serious cases (e.g. Kirsch et al., 2008). There is also the issue of research bias in drug trials and it has been shown that when the research is sponsored by the drug companies it shows a more beneficial effect of the drug than when the research is carried out by people not sponsored by the industry (Lexchin et al., 2003).

The ethical issues that inevitably arise concern the care and welfare of the clients. Is their welfare being put ahead of the commercial interests of the pharmaceutical companies, or is the reverse true?

And are their interests best served with a label for their relatively common behavior?

Happiness

On a lighter note, Bentall (1992) parodied the DSM by proposing that happiness be classified as a mental disorder and be renamed 'major affective disorder: pleasant type'. He suggested that a review of the relevant literature showed that happiness is statistically abnormal, consists of a discrete cluster of symptoms, is associated with a range of cognitive abnormalities and probably reflects the abnormal functioning of the nervous system. The parody highlights the ethical issues that arise from diagnosing more and more of our behaviors as pathological. The diagnosis of everyday behavior as being disordered leads to a growing dependency on the psychology industry – if you have a diagnosis, you obviously need an expert to treat it. This excessive diagnosis also undermines the confidence that people have in their ability to live their lives competently.

Relationships with clients

The issue of sexual involvement between therapist and patients is an obvious area of concern. It is clearly difficult to get accurate data on this topic as people are unlikely to willingly disclose their behavior. Given that, a recent meta-analysis of surveys is quite remarkable. Pope (2001) found that 7% of male therapists and 1.5% of female therapists admitted to sexual intimacies with their clients.

This behavior would appear to be unethical because of the trust that is put in the therapist by the patient. It does not seem likely that therapists can remove themselves totally from the powerful role they have when they take on another role with the patient. So it would appear to be unethical, but is it harmful? Pope and Vetter (1991) published a study of 958 patients who had been sexually involved with a therapist. The findings suggest that about 90% of patients were harmed by sex with a therapist, although this drops slightly to 80% when the sexual involvement begins only after termination of therapy. About 11% required hospitalization, 14% attempted suicide and 1% committed suicide. About 10% had

> ### REFLECTIVE EXERCISE 6.6
>
> Does love conquer all? Think about the various relationships that might be unethical, for example teacher and student, doctor and patient, boss and junior staff member, dinner lady and local butcher. Are these relationships always unethical? If so, why? If not, why not?

experienced rape prior to sexual involvement with the therapist, and about a third had experienced incest or other child sex abuse. About 5% of these patients were minors at the time of the sexual involvement with the therapist. Of those harmed, only 17% recovered fully.

You might argue that it is a fact of life that when people spend time together they sometimes become attracted to each other and sometimes have occasional intimacies, but there is a growing sense that many of these relationships are ethically questionable: the doctor with the patient, the teacher with the student, the boss with the employee, the police officer with the criminal and the vet with the ... well we do not want to go there. All these relationships lead to conflicts of interest and might well harm the very people we are trying to help.

This all seems a sorry state of affairs. Psychologists creating victims, categorizing them, treating them inappropriately and then having sex with them. We hasten to add that we are not suggesting that most or even much of psychological practice is unsound or damaging. We chose to look at this information in order to wrestle with the complex ethical dilemmas faced by professional people when they carry out their work. In theory we can all be the most ethical person in the world, but in everyday life it is not so easy.

Speaking out

Can we avoid ethical dilemmas by keeping quiet? We would argue that psychologists have an ethical and moral responsibility to speak out on some important issues. The ethical problems are related to having to choose when to speak out and having to choose what to say as a psychologist. If we consider military actions, for example, then the UK has been involved in three major conflicts in the last few years: in Kosovo, in Afghanistan and in Iraq. Psychological research has contributed a lot to our understanding about the behavior of armies in warfare, the experience of civilians in warfare and the long-term effects of warfare on military personnel and civilians. Considering that often you cannot switch on the TV without hearing from a psychologist, it is remarkable how silent the profession has been about these military actions.

There has been the occasional article in professional journals (e.g. Sloboda & Coleman, 2000) but little to no comment in the mainstream media. Sloboda (2001) suggests that one of the reasons psychologists give for their silence is the code of conduct that says psychologists should not comment outside their area of specialism and competence. As discussed above in connection with the *Big Brother* psychologists and the TV diagnosticians, psychologists are often happy to stretch this guideline without comment from the profession. Sloboda questions how much competence we need in order to point out the negative effects of warfare, and if we are not competent then do we not have a responsibility to find out about these things? If psychology is the study of mind and behavior, then surely professional bodies such as the British Psychological Society and the American Psychological Association should have something to say about the mind and behavior of military action.

A strange exception to the silence of psychologists over the effects of war and terrorism was the reaction to the destruction of the twin towers in New York on September 11, 2001. Bear in mind that America has the most psychologists anywhere in the world and is the wealthiest country in the world, and then consider that the first official response of the BPS was to offer help and support on behalf of British psychologists to psychologists working in New York with the bereaved and the traumatized. As Sloboda (2001) remarks, is there any city on the planet with more psychologists than New York? The offer appears all the more strange given that no equivalent offer appears to have been made to the citizens of Yugoslavia, Afghanistan or Iraq, who endured months or even years of bombing by Western forces. And if you are uncomfortable with the military side of that dilemma, then look for the offers of psychological support to scenes of natural disasters or famine in the developing world.

Conclusion

This chapter appears to be a stinging critique of psychology, and we have raised some disturbing examples of unethical practice. We think it is important to say that our experience of psychologists is largely very positive and they work with good intentions and in a professional way. What distinguishes psychologists is their very high level of self-criticism (probably their mothers' fault). Also, by way of balance, it is important to note that if we applied the same criteria to virtually any other profession we would find similar dilemmas. For example, in the medical profession there are many dubious relationships between practitioners and pharmaceutical companies, and we do not even know where to start with lawyers or journalists because we would fill the rest of the book. And think about the ethics of a TV presenter such as Gary Lineker, who is paid from public money and uses his position as a child-friendly personality to sell fried salt-covered starch snacks (OK, they are crisps) to children, many of them then need public money to help with obesity issues.

Working with people creates ethical dilemmas for researchers (to ensure that people do not disclose more than they wished; to respect the clients), for individual psychologists (speaking out; selecting their research topics) and for the profession (to speak out or to remain silent; to consider the individual or the wider community). It is easy to take the high moral ground and pick holes in everyone else. We hope we have not done this but have instead given you some reasoned debate on the dilemmas that face psychologists. Where you choose to stand on these dilemmas is up to you.

Summary

Psychologists deal with people in practical ways that can change how they think, feel and behave. These activities bring numerous moral and ethical issues that have to be debated and resolved. In the area of military psychology these debates are not easy to resolve, partly because they are affected by wider moral concerns about the conduct of warfare, for example. Psychologists also have a big presence in the media and their behavior here can have a wide impact on society at large as on well as on the individuals they interact with. In addition psychologists work with people in therapeutic situations and have to deal with difficult issues about what is best for their clients.

FURTHER READING

- Kutchins, H. & Kirk, S. (1997) *Making Us Crazy*. Constable: London. [A readable critique of how the pharmaceutical industry and psychologists create the categories of mental ill *health*.]
- McGuffin, J. (1974). *The Guinea Pigs*. Retrieved from www.irish resistancebooks.com/guineapigs/guineapigs.htm. [The story of the use of psychological techniques by the British Army in Ireland during The Troubles.]
- Ronson, J. (2005) *The Men Who Stare at Goats*. London: Simon & Schuster. [If you want to find out about the interrogation techniques used at Guantanamo, then you could read Jon Ronson's excellent text, or check out some of Ronson's writing on the internet.]

WEBSITES

- World Health Organization site for the ICD
  http://www.who.int/whosis/icd10/
- Ethics website of the American Psychological Association
  http://www.apa.org/ethics/code/index.aspx
- The website of the DSM. Before you read through the material just be aware that everyone who reads through it for the first time thinks they have several of the conditions on the list.
  http://psych.org/MainMenu/Research/DSMIV.aspx

Ethics and your research project

7

What this chapter will teach you

- How ethics are dealt with in universities
- The rights and wrongs of carrying out your own research
- What you need to do to get ethical approval for your project

---

In this chapter we will look at what is required by university departments in order to get ethical approval for your project. We will cover the key issues and provide a checklist of what you need to do.

Your own research

Although this sounds very very obvious, the first thing to do is to decide what it is you want to research. And although it is very obvious, it is not as easy to be clear about this as you would think. It is helpful to break down this question into:

1 What is your main research question?
2 What data will you collect?
3 Whom will you collect your data from?

A research idea often starts with a broad interest in a topic and commonly students say 'I want to do research into serial killers' because they want to know more about an issue that attracts a lot of public interest. A brief moment of reflection will allow you to see why you are very unlikely to be able to do this research. To start with, there are very few serial killers around – think about it and you will realize that if there were loads of serial killers around then there would not be so many of us (non-serial killers) left. Over the last 50 years there have been only around 35 people convicted of serial killing (defined as three or more murders over a time of greater than 30 days) in the UK (Wilson, 2009). True there might have been a few more that have never been found but how would you carry out research on them? Let us cut to the chase – you are not going to get access to any serial killers, so give it up now.

Good, we have put the serial killer research plan in the bin, so what now? If you are starting from an interest in a particular topic or type of behavior or group of people then start to clarify exactly what it is you want to find out. You do not have to consider the three questions above in any particular order but you need to think about all of them.

Participants

Let us look first at the people you might want to study. Lots of people have interesting stories to tell and you might be drawn towards looking at issues of mental distress or extreme behaviors such as drug or alcohol use. Alternatively you might be interested in how children develop and so want to carry out your study with young children.

> ### REFLECTIVE EXERCISE 7.1
>
> Imagine that you want to carry out a research project into the effects of alcoholism. What do you think are the issues you will need to deal with in order to collect data from alcoholics and their families and friends? Take a few moments to think about this before reading on.

The key issues you have to consider when choosing your participants are whether they can provide fully informed consent, whether you can protect their confidentiality and whether the study might bring any emotional or physical harm to them. On top of this you also have to consider whether there are any risks to yourself. You might be quite relaxed about this but the people who have to approve and therefore condone your work will be very concerned about this aspect.

If someone has some mental health issues, they might well consent to your study but will you be able to deal with anything that might arise from your study? If, for example, you are interviewing them, then your questions might provoke a challenging response. This might create problems for your participant or even for you.

Working with children is an activity that is under intense scrutiny due to fears about the motives and activities of some adults. You will need to have a *Criminal Records Check* (CRB) to do even the most basic study and many schools require this of you if you want to carry out any work with their pupils.

We could go on and identify many other special participant groups and the problems you might face in getting ethical approval, but you probably already get the picture. People who have unusual experiences have a special interest for us, but that is not enough reason for you to base your research around them. Having said that, you do not have to give up straight away. You can do research with a wide range of participant groups but you have to be clear of the other two points identified above, as well as safeguarding the participants and yourself.

There is one final point to consider about your choice of participants and that is how you will recruit them. This is more of a practical concern than an ethical one, but you cannot expect that people will be prepared to take part in your study just because you want them to. In fact many people will avoid psychology studies because of the suspicions they have about them and their desire to keep their private life private.

Data

Although this sounds a bit back to front, students sometimes design their research projects around the type of data they want to collect. This is because the main aim of a student project is to showcase research skills rather than to discover new findings. It is about *showing* that you can do science as much as actually *doing* it. Therefore it is a good idea to select the methodology that best shows off your skills of design, data collection and data analysis.

If you want to show off your statistical skills then you will be drawn to studies that collect **quantitative data** and require **analysis of variance** or **regression analyses**, for example. On the other hand if you want to show off your skills of **qualitative analysis** then you will be drawn to interviews or focus groups, for example, and use some type of **thematic analysis**. The route you choose will affect

> ### KEY TERMS
>
> **Quantitative data** Data that represent how much or how long, or how many, etc. there are of something. Data that are measured in numbers or quantities.
>
> **Analysis of variance** A statistical technique for making comparisons of mean scores and estimating the probability of these scores occurring due to chance.
>
> **Qualitative analysis** Summarizing qualitative data i.e. data that represent meanings or anything that cannot be counted. This can be done, for example, by identifying themes and interpreting the meaning of an experience to the individual(s) concerned.
>
> **Thematic analysis** A qualitative method that examines the data repeated to observe themes that occur, based on the strength of the material and its repetition.

the ethical issues you have to deal with, but if you are very clear about what type of data you want to work with then you may need to adjust your research questions or your participants to allow you to do this.

For example, you might be very interested in looking at issues around obsessive–compulsive disorder (OCD) and you want to show off your interview skills. It might be difficult to recruit a group of people with OCD and even more difficult to be able to provide sufficient safeguards to get ethical approval. However, it might be easier to recruit people who have experience of people with OCD, for example family members or friends, and if you choose to talk to these people the safeguarding issues will be much easier to deal with. You are still able to deal with an interesting issue, and the impact of OCD (and other mental health issues) on family members is an important and relatively little studied area.

The quantitative approach often creates less in the way of safe-guarding issues. Questionnaire studies are commonly quite imperson-al and the main concern is about the confidentiality of the data and the right to withdraw date from the data set. These are usually manage-able issues. Studies with participants in laboratories can create some special issues, although the most common one is boredom.

The important thing is to precisely identify what data you will collect and how you will go about collecting it. You need to consider what impact the collection of these data will have on your participants and also on yourself. You also need to be very clear about how you can ensure the confidentiality of the people included in the study, so, for example, using a shared computer to store your data would be an obvious problem here.

Research question

Most purists will say that you should start with the research question, but then they would. Thinking about your research after you have decided on who you are going to study and what data you are going to collect sounds very back to front but it is also a very practical way of preparing for your research project. It is also not as uncommon as you might be led to believe. However, whenever you decide to think about it you still have to come up with a clear research question.

The research question and design is often the first thing you have to put on your *ethics approval form*. So, although you came to this part of the process last you have to show a clear line of thought that starts with a question and moves to your planned method and analysis. This research question needs to be precise and also within the scope of project you intend to carry out.

Another issue to think about is who owns the study you are planning. You are likely to think that it is your study and only yours, but you would be wrong. Imagine you carry out a study that the university would not approve of or a study that might create negative headlines. Maybe you show violent videos to children to measure the impact of the videos on aggression scores, and later that evening one of the children bites the head off a whippet and says he was only copying what he saw during the psychology study. Your university would, quite rightly, be given a very public kicking for allowing you to carry that out as part of one of their courses.

Your study needs to be carried out in a responsible way and you need to ensure that you have considered as many of the possible outcomes as possible. Although this might seem a little restrictive on you it also provides a lot of support as well. If you have been through the ethics procedure and you have carried out the study as you said you would, then even if something goes hideously wrong (such as decapitated whippets) you will be supported by your tutors and university.

Not a done deal

Ethics are not cut and dried and the best way to sort out the ethics of your particular study is to discuss them with your peers and your tutor. Think about the issues we have briefly introduced above, the checklist of questions we have produced below and also use your own good judgement.

Key questions to ask when writing your ethics statement for your project

The following may look like a very long list of questions to consider when designing your study and preparing your *ethics approval form*, but it represents a summary of several forms we have looked at and is actually shorter than any of them.

Design

- What is the title of the project?
- What are the main objectives of the study?
- What are the details of any psychometric tests that will be used?

Participant selection

- Who are the participants?
- How will they be recruited?
- What will the participants be asked to do?
- How long will the participants be required to be involved in the data collection?
- How many participants will be recruited?
- Could the participants be considered a vulnerable group?
  - Does the project involve direct contact with children or young people under 18 years of age?
  - Does the project involve direct contact with adults with learning difficulties; adults who are infirm or physically disabled; adults who are resident in social care or medical establishments; or adults in the custody of the criminal justice system?
  - Has a CRB check been stipulated as a condition of access to any source of data required for the project?

Sensitive research

Does the research involve the possible disclosure of sensitive or criminal activities? For example:

- Is there a significant risk that the project will lead participants to disclose evidence that children or vulnerable adults are being harmed or are at risk of harm?
- Might people disclose evidence of previous criminal offences, or their intention to commit criminal offences, in the course of the research?
- Does the research involve 'sensitive' information, that is, information about individuals' religious beliefs, political opinions, sexual orientation or behavior, mental or physical health, financial affairs, trade union membership or involvement in criminal proceedings?

Risk of physical or emotional harm

Is there a significant risk that the research may lead to:

- physical harm to the participants or the researchers?
- significant psychological or emotional distress to the participants or the researchers?
- damage to the reputation of the university, the researchers, the participants or any partner organizations such as employers?

Informed consent

- What information will be given to the participants before they are asked for their consent?
- Will formal written consent be asked for?
- If the data are being collected via the internet, how will informed consent be ensured?
- How will the participants be informed of their right to withdraw during the study and the right to subsequently withdraw their data?
- Will data collection take place in situations where the participant might not feel able to give informed independent consent, such as a prison or a classroom?
- Will the participants be given any inducements to take part, such as money or course credits?

Safeguarding researchers and participants

- Is there a significant risk that the study could induce stress or discomfort beyond that which a participant would expect in everyday life?
- Does the research involve invasive or potentially harmful procedures (such as poking people with a pointed stick)?
- Is there a risk that the situations in which data are being collected could threaten the safety of the participants or the researchers?

Data protection

- Will any part of the research involve audio or film recording of individuals?
- How will the confidentiality of participants be protected?
- Who will be entitled to have access to the raw data? What steps have been taken to ensure that only entitled persons will have access to the data?
- How and where will the data be stored, in what format and for how long?
- How will the data be disposed of at the end of the project?
- How will the results of the research be used?
- Is there a significant possibility that any of your participants, or people associated with them, could be directly or indirectly identified in the outputs from this project?
- What feedback about their own data or about the overall study results will be given to participants?

The above gives a flavor of the range of ethical issues you will have to deal with when designing your own project. It covers most of the major areas but not all of the details. As we said above, for the fine tuning of your own approval form you need to trust your own good judgement to consider all the potential hazards.

Summary

This chapter has summarized the major ethical issues for you to consider when designing your own studies. There are a number of principles to consider but in the end each study has its own unique set of issues that have to be considered and dealt with.

Glossary

Absolutist morals. The view that some things are simply right or wrong; there is no relative position. For example, murder is wrong no matter what the circumstances are.

Analysis of variance. A statistical technique for making comparisons of mean scores and estimating the probability of these scores occurring due to chance.

Autism. A socially disabling disorder that usually appears in early childhood and typically involves avoidance of social contact, abnormal language development and 'stereotypical' or bizarre behaviors such as rocking.

Behaviorist. The view that all behavior can be explained in terms of learning theory (classical and operant conditioning), referring only to the behaviors themselves rather than any internal mechanisms in order to explain behavior.

Case study. A research method that involves a detailed study of a single individual, institution or event, and usually involves a variety of different methods such as interviews and psychological tests.

Cognitive developmental. An approach that focuses on how our behavior is influenced by the cognitive (mental) changes that take place as a person grows older, such as changes in memory, perceptual or intellectual abilities.

Confederate. An individual in a study who is not a real participant and has been instructed how to behave by the investigator/experimenter.

Confidentiality. A participant's right to have personal information protected. The Data Protection Act makes this a legal right.

Consent. Giving your agreement to participate. A distinction is made between 'consent' and 'informed consent' where agreement is based on having comprehensive information concerning the nature and purpose of a study and the participant's role in it.

Controlled observation. A form of investigation in which behavior is observed but under controlled conditions, as opposed to a naturalistic observation.

Cross-cultural research. A kind of natural experiment in which the independent variable is different cultural practices and the dependent variable is a behavior such as attachment. This enables researchers to investigate the effects of culture/socialization.

Debriefing. A post-research interview designed to inform the participant of the true nature of the study, and to restore them to the same state they were in at the start of the experiment. It may also be used to gain useful feedback about the procedures in the study. There are some who claim that debriefing is *not* an *ethical issue* but a means of dealing with ethical issues. However, it could be argued that *lack* of debriefing is an ethical issue in the same way that it is only the lack of informed consent that is the ethical issue.

Deception. This occurs when a participant is not told the true aims of a study (e.g. what participation will involve), thus the participants cannot give truly informed consent. Deception may be active (e.g. the participant is given false information) or passive (e.g. information is withheld).

Demand characteristics. A cue that makes participants aware of what the researcher expects to find or how participants are expected to behave.

Deontological perspective. An approach to morality based on the idea of obligation or duty. Deontology is not necessarily an absolutist position because some deontologists believe it is morally acceptable to disobey a rule if the consequences are bad, such as refusing to tell the truth if it will harm someone.

Dependent variable (DV). The DV depends in some way on the independent variable (IV). The DV is measured in some way to assess the effects of the IV.

Determinist. The view that an individual's behavior is shaped or controlled by internal or external forces rather than an individual's will to do something.

Diagnostic and Statistical Manual of Mental Disorders. The categorization and description of mental disorders. It is published by the American Psychiatric Association and is widely used in the USA, and to varying degrees around the world, by diagnosticians and policy-makers.

Dissociative disorders. Mental disorders where the patient experiences dissociation from or interruption of 'normal' waking functions such as memory (amnesia) or identity (multiple personality disorder, now called dissociative identity disorder, where a person has multiple identities).

Ecological validity. The ability to generalize a research effect, beyond the particular setting in which it is demonstrated, to other settings.

Equipoise. An important principle in medical research that there should be equal benefit offered in both experimental conditions (called 'arms') in a clinical trial.

Ethical committee (also called an Institutional Review Board, IRB). A group of people within a research institution that must approve a study before it begins. Such committees usually consist of lay members as well as professionals from the research institution.

Ethical issues. These arise in research where there are conflicts between the research goals and the participant's rights.

Ethical relativism. The view that there are no objective, universal morals; they are all relative to time and place.

Ethics. The rules and principles that distinguish between right and wrong, and guide our behavior.

Ethnocentrism. Believing that one's own ingroup (e.g. religious group, nation, culture to which you belong) is superior to other groups.

Ethnography. A method of participant observation used by sociologists and anthropologists to study daily life at first-hand.

Experiment. A research method to investigate causal relationships by observing the effect of an independent variable on the dependent variable.

Explicit and implicit memory. A way to classify different kinds of memory, distinguishing between memories of which we are aware (explicit) and those memories that are outside our conscious awareness (implicit).

Field study. Any study that is conducted outside a laboratory (i.e. not in a specially designed environment); this includes field experiments, naturalistic observations and case studies.

Imposed etic. A technique or theory that is developed in one culture and then used to study the behavior of people in other cultures.

Independent variable. Some event that is directly manipulated by an experimenter in order to test its effect on another variable (the dependent variable).

Informed consent. The agreement given by an individual to participate in a research study or any program, based on comprehensive information concerning the nature and purpose of the study or program and their role in it. This is necessary so that they can make an informed decision about whether to participate.

Laboratory. A specially constructed environment where conditions can be carefully controlled.

Learned helplessness. When an animal finds that its responses are ineffective, it learns that there is no point in responding and behaves passively in future.

Microdosing. Technique for studying the behavior of drugs in humans through the administration of doses so low that they are unlikely to produce whole-body effects but high enough to allow the cellular response to be studied.

Morals. Rules of right and wrong to guide our behavior based on socially agreed principles. Ethics are a moral framework that is applied to a narrow group of people such as doctors or psychologists.

Mundane realism. Refers to how a study mirrors the real world. The experimental environment is realistic to the degree to which experiences encountered in the experimental environment will occur in everyday life (the 'real world').

Natural experiment. A research method in which the experimenter cannot manipulate the independent variable directly, but where it varies naturally, and the effect on a dependent variable can be observed.

Netnography (also called online ethnography). The use of material that is publically available on the internet for research purposes (often for consumer research). The term is derived from 'ethnography'.

Nuremberg Defense. A plea in a court of law that someone, most commonly a soldier, cannot be held responsible for their behavior because they were following orders.

Placebo. A dummy medical (or other) treatment given to assess the psychological effects of the treatment, i.e. the belief that the treatment is beneficial.

Post-traumatic stress disorder. An anxiety disorder resulting from experience with a catastrophic event beyond the normal range of human suffering, and characterized by numbness to the world, reliving the trauma in dreams and memories and symptoms of anxiety.

Presumptive consent. A method of dealing with lack of informed consent or deception by asking a group of people who are similar to the participants whether they would agree to take part in a study. If this group of people consent to the procedures in the proposed study, it is *presumed* that the real participants would agree as well.

Prior general consent. Prospective participants in a research study are asked if they would take part in certain kinds of research, including ones involving deception. If they say yes, they have given their general consent to taking part in such research.

Privacy. A person's right to control the flow of information about themselves.

Psychoanalytic. Freud's explanation of how adult personality develops as a consequence of the interaction between biological (sexual) drives and early experience.

Qualitative analysis. Summarizing qualitative data, that is, data that represent meanings or anything that cannot be counted. This can be done, for example, by identifying themes and interpreting the meaning of an experience to the individual(s) concerned.

Quantitative data. Data that represent how much, how long, how many, etc. there are of something. Data that are measured in numbers or quantities.

Quasi-experiment. Studies that are 'almost' experiments but lack one or more features of a true experiment, such as full experimenter control over the independent variable and/or random allocation of participants to conditions. This means that such studies cannot claim to demonstrate causal relationships.

Race science. Commonly refers to the various attempts to cover racist ideas with a gloss of scientific respectability. The science is invariably poor and the conclusions are still racist.

Recovered Memory Therapy. A term used to describe a range of psychiatric techniques based on recalling memories of childhood experiences that had been forgotten. The techniques are very controversial because the balance of evidence is that unpleasant experiences cannot be completely repressed and forgotten, and false memories can be easily created during therapy.

Regression analysis. A statistical technique to measure the relationship between two or more variables. It is used to estimate how far one of the variables (the dependent variable) can be predicted using data from the other variables (the independent variables).

Relativist morals. The view that morals are not absolute but are dependent on context; for example, in some situations stealing is acceptable. The intrinsic 'wrongness' of an act may be overridden by other considerations.

Right to withdraw. The right of participants to refuse to continue with participation in a study if they are uncomfortable in any way, and to refuse permission for the researcher to use any data produced before they withdraw.

Sensory deprivation. The cutting out of all incoming sensory information, or at least as much of it as possible. Sometimes used as a method of torture.

Sentience. Being able to sense and feel, and also a subjective awareness of those sensations. For example, sentience is more than just reacting to pain but also a conscious awareness of pain.

Socially sensitive research. Any research that might have direct social consequences.

Speciesism. A term coined by the psychologist Richard D. Ryder in 1970. It is the assumption that some individuals are superior based solely on the grounds that they are members of the species *Homo Sapiens*. Speciesism is similar to sexism or racism – where superiority is defined by sex or race.

Strange Situation technique. Method to assess strength of attachment, conducted in a novel environment and involving eight episodes. An infant's behavior is observed as mother leaves and returns, and when with a stranger.

Subject of a life. A way to describe the fact that some animals are more than merely alive and conscious. Subjects of a life are characterized by a set of features including having beliefs, feelings, memory and self-awareness.

Thematic analysis. A qualitative method that examines the data repeated to observe themes that occur, based on the strength of the material and its repetition.

Undisclosed (covert) and disclosed (overt) observations. Observing people without their knowledge, for example using one-way mirrors, or observing people with their knowledge, which may alter the way they behave.

Utilitarian approach. A theoretical framework for morality where decisions about what is right or wrong are based on the principle of what is useful or practical for the most people. See page 121.

Utilitarianism. A theoretical framework for morality where decisions about what is right or wrong are based on the principle of what is useful or practical for the majority of people; established by weighing costs and benefits for individuals and society.

References

Abramson, L.Y., Metalsky, F.I. & Alloy, L.B. (1989) Hopelessness depression: A theory based subtype of depression. *Psychological Review, 96*(2), 358–372.

American Psychological Association (2002a) *Guidelines on Multicultural Education, Training, Research, Practice, and Organisational Change for Psychologists.* Retrieved June 2010 from http://www.apa.org/pi/oema/resources/policy/multicultural-guidelines.aspx

American Psychological Association (2002b) Ethical principles for psychologists and code of conduct. *American Psychologist, 57*, 1060–1073.

APA Ethics Committee (2009) *No Defense to Torture under the APA Ethics Code.* Retrieved September 2010 from http://www.apa.org/news/press/statements/ethics-statement-torture.pdf

APS (2001) *William James Fellow Award.* Retrieved February 2011 from http://www.psychologicalscience.org/awards/james/citations/loftus.html

Atkinson, R.C. & Shiffrin, R.M. (1968) Human memory: A proposed system and its control processes. In K.W. Spence and J.T. Spence (Eds.), *The Psychology of Learning and Motivation* (Vol. 2, pp. 742–775). London: Academic Press.

Banks, M.S., Aslin, R.N. & Weiskopf, S. (1975) Sensitive period for the development of human binocular vision. *Science, 190*, 675–677.

Banyard, P. & Hunt, N. (2000) Reporting research: Something missing? *The Psychologist, 13*(2), 68–71.

Baron, R.A. & Byrne, D. (1991) *Social Psychology: Understanding Human Interactions* (6th edition). Boston: Allyn & Bacon.

Baumrind, D. (1964) Some thoughts on ethics of research: After reading Milgram's behavioral study of obedience. *American Psychologist, 19*, 421–423.

Bentall, R. P. (1992) A proposal to classify happiness as a psychiatric disorder. *Journal of Medical Ethics, 18*(2), 94–98.

Bickman, L. (1974) Clothes make the person. *Psychology Today, 8*(4), 48–51.

Big Brother (2000) Retrieved June 2010 from bigbrother.digitalspy.co.uk/article/ds419.html

Blakemore, C. & Cooper, G.F. (1970) Development of the brain depends on the visual environment. *Nature, 228*, 477–478.

Bloche M.G. & Marks, J.H. (2005) Doctors and interrogators at Guantanamo Bay. *New England Journal of Medicine, 353*(1), 6–8.

Booth, W.C. (1974) *Modern Dogma and the Rhetoric of Assent* (Vol. 5), Ward-Phillips lectures in English language and literature. Chicago: University of Chicago Press.

Bouhoutsos, J.C., Goodchilds, J.D. & Huddy, L. (1986) Media psychology: An empirical study of radio call-in psychology programs. *Professional Psychology: Research and Practice, 17*(5), 408–414.

Boyle, E. (2009) Neuroscience and animal sentience. Guest article for *Compassion in World Farming*. Retrieved February 2009 from http://www.ciwf.org.uk/includes/documents/cm_docs/2009/b/boyle_2009_neuro science_and_animal_sentience.pdf

British Psychological Society (2006) What's the worst idea on the mind? *The Psychologist, 19*, 518–519.

British Psychological Society (2007) *Guidelines for Psychologists Working with Animals*. Retrieved February 2011 from http://www.bps.org.uk/downloadfile. cfm?file_uuid=DA9509C9-1143-DFD0-7EE7-9D998D01F023&ext=pdf

British Psychological Society (2009a) *Code of Ethics and Conduct*. Retrieved February 2011 from http://www.bps.org.uk/the-society/code-of-conduct/

British Psychological Society (2009b) *Conducting Research on the Internet: Guidelines for Ethical Practice in Psychological Research Online*. Retrieved February 2011 from http://www.bps.org.uk/document-download-area/document-download$.cfm?file_uuid=2B3429B3-1143-DFD0-7E5A-4BE3FDD763CC&ext=pdf

Brownell, K.D. & Foreyt, J. (1986) *Handbook of Eating Disorders: Physiology, Psychology and the Treatment of Obesity, Anorexia and Bulimia*. London: Harper Collins.

BUAV (British Union for the Abolition of Vivesection) (2010) *What's Wrong with Animal Experiments (A Guide for Students)*. London: BUAV.

Butler, E. (2009) *Mobile Phone-Tapping*. Retrieved February 2010 from http://www.adamsmith.org/blog/justice-and-civil-liberties/mobile-phone%11tapping-200904153316/

Canadian Psychological Association, Sindair, C. & Pettifor, J. (Eds.) (2001) *Companion Manual to the Canadian Code of Ethics for Psychologists* (3rd edition). Ottawa, Ontario: Canadian Psychological Association.

Canter, D. & Breakwell, G. (1986) Psychologists and "the media". *Bulletin of the British Psychological Society, 39*, 281–286.

Charlton, T., Gunter, B. & Hannan, A. (Eds.) (2000) *Broadcast Television Effects in a Remote Community*, Hillsdale, NJ: Lawrence Erlbaum Associates.

Christiansen, L. (1988) Deception in psychological research: When is its use justified? *Personality and Social Psychology Bulletin, 14*, 664–675.

CIWF (2010) *The Science of Animal Sentience*. Retrieved June 2010 from http://www.ciwf.org.uk/animal_sentience/science/default.aspx

Clarke-Carter, D. (1997) The account taken of statistical power in research. *British Journal of Psychology, 88*, 71–83.

Colby, A. & Kohlberg, L. (1987) *The Measurement of Moral Judgement. Volume I: Theoretical Formulations and Research Validation. Volume II: Standard Issue Scoring Manual.* Cambridge: Cambridge University Press.

Colman, A.M. (1987) *Facts, Fallacies and Frauds in Psychology.* London: Unwin Hyman.

Corkin, S.M. (1984) Lasting consequences of bilateral medial temporal lobectomy: Clinical course and experimental findings in H.M. *Seminars in Neurology, 4,* 249–259.

Daeg de Mott, D. K. (2001) Ethics. *Gale Encyclopedia of Psychology.* Retrieved February 2011 from http://www.findarticles.com/p/articles/mi_g2699/is_0004/ai_2699000457/

Daily Mail (2009, August) Retrieved June 2010 from http://www.dailymail.co.uk/news/worldnews/article-1230814/Forget-Seals-meet-Navy-Sea-Lions-Animals-clear-mines-fight-terrorists.html

Deaux, K. (1984) From individual difference to social categories: Analysis of a decade's research on gender. *American Psychologist, 39,* 105–116.

Department of Health (2004) *Prescription Cost Analysis England 2003.* Retrieved February, 2011 from http://www.dh.gov.uk/en/Publicationsandstatistics/Statistics/StatisticalWorkAreas/Statisticalhealthcare/DH_4086603

Dineen, T. (1999) *Manufacturing Victims: What the Psychology Industry Is Doing to People.* London: Constable & Robinson.

Dunayer, J. (2002) *Animal Equality.* Retrieved May 2004 from http://www.upc-online.org/thinking/animal_equality.html

Dweck, C.S. (1975) The role of expectations and attributions in the alleviation of learned helplessness. *Journal of Personality and Social Psychology, 31,* 674–685.

Eagle, N., Pentland, A.S. & Lazer, D. (2009) Inferring friendship network structure by using mobile phone data. *Proceedings of the National Academy of Sciences, 106*(36), 15274–15278.

Edwards, R. (1993) An education in interviewing: Placing the researcher and the research. In R. Lee and C. Renzetti (Eds.), *Researching Sensitive Topics* (pp. 181–196). London: Sage.

Eysenck, H.J. (1991) *Smoking, Personality and Stress.* New York: Springer-Verlag.

Festinger, L., Riecken, H.W. & Schachter, S. (1956) *When Prophecy Fails.* Minneapolis: University of Minneapolis Press.

Field, A.P. & Lawson, J. (2003) Fear information and the development of fears during childhood: Effects on implicit fear responses and behavioral avoidance. *Behavior Research and Therapy, 41,* 1277–1293.

Florian, V. & Mikulincer, M. (1998) Symbolic immortality and the management of the terror of death: The moderating role of attachment style. *Journal of Personality and Social Psychology, 74,* 725–734.

Frank, E. (1983) Psychology at six: Presenting psychological information to a mass audience in a news format. *Clinical Psychologist, 36*(2), 35–37.

Freud, S. (1973) *The New Introductory Lectures on Psychoanalysis.* Harmondsworth, Middlesex: Penguin.

Fukuyama, F. (2001) Natural rights and human history. *The National Interest, 64,* 19–30.

Gamson, W.B., Fireman, B. & Rytina, S. (1982) *Encounters with Unjust Authority.* Homewood, IL: Dorsey Press.

Gardner, B.T. & Gardner, R.A. (1969) Teaching sign language to a chimpanzee. *Science, 165,* 664–672.

Gray, J.A. (1991) On the morality of speciesism. *The Psychologist, 14,* 196–198.

Green, S. (1994) *Principles of Biopsychology,* Hove, UK: Lawrence Erlbaum Associates.

Greenberg, M. (1967) Role-playing: An alternative to deception? *Journal of Personality and Social Psychology, 7,* 152–157.

Halkitis, P.N., Parsons, J.T. & Wilton, L. (2003) Barebacking among gay and bisexual men in New York City: explanations for the emergence of intentional unsafe behavior. *Archives of Sexual Behavior, 32,* 351–357.

Harlow, H.F (1959) Love in infant monkeys. *Scientific American, 200*(6), 68–74.

Haslam, A. & Reicher, S. (2003) A tale of two prison experiments: Beyond a role-based explanation of tyranny. *Psychology Review, 9*(4), 2–6.

Health and Social Care Information Centre (2009) *Prescription Cost Analysis England 2008.* Retrieved September 2010 from http://www.ic.nhs.uk/pubs/prescostanalysis2008

Hebb, D.O., Heron, W. & Bexton, W.H. (1952) The effect of isolation upon attitude, motivation and thought. *Fourth Canadian Defence Research Board, Symposium: Military Medicine 1,* in cooperation with McGill University, Ottawa, Canada.

Heider, F. (1958) *The Psychology of Interpersonal Relations.* New York: Wiley.

Hewstone, M., Stroebe, W., Codol, J.P. & Stephenson, G. (1988) *Introduction to Social Psychology: A European Perspective.* Oxford: Blackwell.

Hilts, P. (1995) *Memory's Ghost: The Strange Tale of Mr. M. and the Nature of Memory.* New York: Simon & Schuster.

Home Office (2000) *Guidance on the Operation of the Animals (Scientific Procedures) Act 1986.* London: The Stationery Office.

House of Lords Select Committee on Animals (2002) *Scientific Procedures Report.* London: The Stationery Office.

Hubel, D.H. & Wiesel, T.N. (1962) Receptive fields, binocular interaction and functional architecture in the cat's visual cortex. *Journal of Physiology, 160,* 106–154.

Hubel, D.H. & Wiesel, T.N. (1970) The period of susceptibility to the physiological effects of unilateral eye closure in kittens. *Journal of Physiology, 206,* 419–436.

Hubel, D.H.,Wiesel, T.N. & LeVay, S. (1977) Plasticity of ocular dominance columns in monkey striate cortex. *Philosophical Transactions of the Royal Society of London, Series B, 278,* 377–409.

Humphreys, L. (1970) *Tearoom Trade: A Study of Homosexual Encounters in Public Places*. Chicago: Aldine.

Jones, J.M. (1991) Psychological models of race: What have they been and what should they be? In J. D. Goodchilds (Ed.), *Psychological Perspectives on Human Diversity in America* (pp. 3–45). Washington: American Psychological Association.

Jouvet, M. (1967) Mechanisms of the states of sleep: A neuropharmological approach. *Research Publications of the Association for the Research in Nervous and Mental Disorders*, 45, 86–126.

Joynson, R.B. (1989) *The Burt Affair*. London: Routledge.

Kamin, L. (1974) *The Science and Politics of IQ*. Harmondsworth: Penguin.

Katz, J. (1972) *Experimentation with Human Beings*. New York: Russell Sage Foundation.

Keith-Spiegel, P. & Koocher, G.P. (1985) *Ethics in Psychology*. Oxford: Oxford University Press.

Kilkenny, C., Parsons, N., Kadyszewski, E., Festing, F.W., Cuthill, I.C., Fry, D., Hutton, J., & Altman, D.G. (2009) Survey of the quality of experimental design, statistical analysis and reporting of research using animals. *PLoS ONE*, 4(11).

Kimmel, A.J. (1996) *Ethical Issues in Behavioral Research*. Oxford: Blackwell.

Kimmel, A.J. (2007) *Ethical Issues in Behavioral Research* (2nd edition). Oxford: Blackwell.

Kinsey, A.C., Pomeroy, W.B. & Martin, C.E. (1948) *Sexual Behavior in the Human Male*. Philadelphia: Saunders.

Kirsch, I., Deacon, B.J., Huedo-Medina, T.B., Scoboria, A., Moore, T.J. & Johnson, B.T. (2008) Initial severity and antidepressant benefits: A meta-analysis of data submitted to the Food and Drug Administration. *PLoS Med*, 5(2), e45.

Kitzinger, C. (1998) Challenging gender biases: Feminist psychology at work. *Psychology Review*, 4, 18–20.

Kline, P. (1991) *Intelligence: The Psychometric View*. London: Routledge.

Kohlberg, L. (1978) Revisions in the theory and practice of moral development. *Directions for Child Development*, 2, 83–88.

Kutchins, H. & Kirk, S. (1997) *Making Us Crazy*. London: Constable.

Landis, C. (1924) Studies of emotional reactions: II. General behavior and facial expression. *Journal of Comparative Psychology*, 4, 447–509.

Lee, R.M. (1993) *Doing Research on Sensitive Topics*. London: Sage.

Levant, R. (2007) Visit to the U.S. Joint Task Force Station at Guantanamo Bay: A first-person account. *Military Psychology*, 19(1), 1–7.

Levin, P. & Arluke, A. (1985) An exploratory analysis of sex differences in gossip. *Sex Roles*, 12, 281–286.

LeVine, R.A. & Campbell, D.T. (1972) *Ethnocentrism: Theories of Conflict, Ethnic Attitudes and Group Behavior*. New York: Wiley.

Lexchin, J., Bero, L., Djulbegovic, B. & Clark, O. (2003) Pharmaceutical industry sponsorship and research outcome and quality: Systematic review. *British Medical Journal*, 326, 1167.

Lifton, R.J. (2004) Doctors and torture. *New England Journal of Medicine, 351*, 415–441.

Lilly, J.C. (1956) Mental effects of reduction of ordinary levels of physical stimuli on intact healthy persons. *Psychological Research Reports, 5*, 1–9.

Loftus, E. (2000) The most dangerous book you may already be reading. *Psychology Today, 84*, 32–35.

Martelle, J.L., Czoty, P.W. & Nader, M.A. (2008) Effect of time-out duration on the reinforcing strength of cocaine assessed under a progressive-ratio schedule in rhesus monkeys. *Behavioral Pharmacology, 19*, 743–746.

Matlin, M.W. (1987) *The Psychology of Women*. London: Holt, Rinehart & Winston.

McCoy, A.W. (2007) Science in Dachau's shadow: Hebb, Beecher, and the development of CIA psychological torture and modern medical ethics. *Journal of the History of the Behavioral Sciences, 43*(4), 401–417.

McGuffin, J. (1974) *The Guinea Pigs*. Retrieved February 2011 from www.irishresistancebooks.com/guineapigs/guineapigs.htm

Milgram, S. (1963) Behavioral study of obedience. *Journal of Abnormal and Social Psychology, 67*, 371–378.

Milgram, S. (1974) *Obedience to Authority: An Experimental View*. New York: Harper & Row.

Miller, G. (1969) Psychology as a means of promoting human welfare. *American Psychologist, 24*, 1063–1075.

Miller, W. & Seligman, M.E.P. (1974) Depression and learned helplessness in man. *Journal of Abnormal Psychology, 84*, 228–238.

Moore, H.T. (1922). Further data concerning sex differences. *Journal of Abnormal and Social Psychology, 17*, 210–214.

Morgan, E. (1995) Measuring time with a biological clock. *Biological Sciences Review, 7*, 2–5.

New York Daily News (2008) Dr. Phil sez Britney Spears needs 'psychological intervention'. Retrieved September 2010 from http://www.nydailynews.com/gossip/2008/01/05/2008-01-05_dr_phil_sez_britney_spears_needs_psychol.html

Nobles, W. (1976) Extended self: Rethinking the so-called Negro self concept. *Journal of Black Psychology, 2*, 15–24.

Nosek, B.A., Banaji, M.R. & Greenwald, A.G. (2002) E-research: Ethics, security, design, and control in psychological research on the internet. *Journal of Social Issues, 58*, 161–176.

Ogden, J.A. & Corkin, S. (1991) Memories of H.M. In W.C. Abraham, M.C. Corballis & K.G. White (Eds.), *Memory Mechanisms: A Tribute to G.V. Goddard* (pp. 195–215). Hillsdale, NJ: Lawrence Erlbaum Associates.

Olds, J. & Milner, P. (1954) Positive reinforcement produced by electrical stimulation of the septal area and other regions of the rat brain. *Journal of Comparative and Physiological Psychology, 47*, 419–428.

Orwell, G. (1949) *Nineteen Eighty-Four*. London: Secker & Warburg.

Ouseley, H. (2001) *Community Pride not Prejudice*. Making Diversity Work in Bradford, Bradford Race Review, Bradford Council. Retrieved June 2005 from http://wwwBradford2020.com/pride/

Parkin, A.J. (1996) H.M.: The medial temporal lobes and memory. In C. Code, C.W. Wallesch, Y. Joanette & A.B. Lecours (Eds.), *Classic Cases in Neuropsychology* (pp. 337–348). London: Psychology Press.

PETA (2010) *Doesn't the Law Protect Animals from Cruelty?* Retrieved June 2010 from http://www.peta.org/about/faq-viv.asp

Piliavin, I., Rodin, J. & Piliavin, J. (1969) Good Samaritanism: An underground phenomenon? *Journal of Personality and Social Psychology, 13*, 289–299.

Plous, S. (1996) Attitudes toward the use of animals in psychological research and education: Results from a national survey of psychology majors. *Psychological Science, 7*, 352–358.

Pope, K. (2001) Sex between therapists and clients. In J. Worell (Ed.), *Encyclopedia of Women and Gender: Sex Similarities and Differences and the Impact of Society on Gender* (pp. 955–962). New York: Academic Press.

Pope, K. & Gutheil, T. (2009) The interrogation of detainees: How doctors' and psychologists' ethical policies differ. *British Medical Journal, 338*, 1178–1180.

Pope, K. & Vetter, V.A. (1991) Prior therapist–patient sexual involvement among patients seen by psychologists. *Psychotherapy, 28*(3), 429–438.

Ramsey, S. (2001) Audit further exposes UK's worst serial killer. *Lancet, 357*, 123–124.

Rapoff, M.A. (1980) Suppression of self-injurious behavior: Determining the least restrictive alternative. *Journal of Mental Deficiency Research, 24*, 37–42.

Raviv, A., Raviv, A. & Yunovitz, R. (1989) Radio psychology and psychotherapy: Comparison of client attitudes and expectations. *Professional Psychology: Research and Practice, 20*(2), 67–72.

Regan, T. (1984) *Empty Cages: Facing the Challenge of Animal Rights*. Lanham, MD: Rowman & Littlefield.

Reicher, S. & Haslam, A. (2009) FORUM: The real world. *The Psychologist, 22*(6), 469.

Richelson, J.T. (2008) *Signals Intelligence*. Retrieved February 2011 from http://www.euronet.nl/~rembert/echelon/usic08.htm

Riesen, A.H. (1956) Effects of early deprivation of photic stimulation. In S. Oster and R. Cook (Eds.), *The Biosocial Basis of Mental Retardation* (pp. 61–85). Baltimore: Johns Hopkins University Press.

Ronson, J. (2005) *The Men Who Stare at Goats*. London: Simon & Schuster.

Rose, S.C., Bisson, J., Churchill, R. & Wessely, S. (2009) *Psychological Debriefing for Preventing Post Traumatic Stress Disorder (PTSD) (Review)*. The Cochrane Collaboration. New York: Wiley.

Rosenhan, D.L. (1973) On being sane in insane places. *Science, 179*, 250–258.

Rosenthal, R. & Fode, K.L. (1963) The effect of experimenter bias on the performance of the albino rat. *Behavioral Science, 8*(3), 183–189.

Rousseau, J.J. (1999) *Discourse on the Origin of Inequality*. Oxford: Oxford University Press. (Original work published 1754)

Rowland, M. (2005) Microdosing and the 3Rs. Retrieved February 2010 from http://www.nc3rs.org.uk/news.asp?id=193

Rubin, G.J., Brewin, C.R., Greenberg, N. & Wessely, S. (2005) Psychological and behavioral reactions to the bombings in London on 7 July 2005: Cross sectional survey of a representative sample of Londoners. *British Medical Journal, 331*, 606.

Rushton, J. (1990) Race differences, r/K theory and a reply to Flynn. *The Psychologist, 5*, 195–198.

Russell, W.M.S. & Burch, R. (1959) *The Principles of Humane Experimental Technique*. London: Methuen.

Rutter, M., Colvert, E., Kreppner, J., Beckett, C., Castle, J., Grootheus, C., Hawkins, A., Stevens, S.E. & Sonuga-Barke, E.J.S. (2007) Early adolescent outcomes for institutionally-deprived and non-deprived adoptees. I: disinhibited attachment. *Journal of Child Psychology and Psychiatry, 48*, 17–30.

Rymer, R. (1993) *Genie – Escape from a Silent Childhood*. London: Michael Joseph.

Schachter, S. (1959) *The Psychology of Affiliation*. Stanford, CA: Stanford University Press.

Schulz, F. (2000) *The Humanist Basis for Human Rights*. Retrieved February 2011 from http://findarticles.com/p/articles/mi_m1374/is_s_60/ai_65133034/

Seligman, M.E.P. (1975) *Helplessness: On Depression, Development and Death*. San Francisco: W.H. Freeman.

Seligman, M.E.P. & Maier, S.F. (1967) Failure to escape traumatic shock. *Journal of Experimental Psychology, 74*, 1–9.

Seyfarth, D.M. & Cheney, D.L. (1980) The ontogeny of vervet monkey alarm calling behavior: A preliminary report. *Zeitschrift für Tierpsychologie, 54*, 37–56.

Shallice, T. (1972) The Ulster depth interrogation techniques and their relation to sensory deprivation research. *Cognition, 1*(4), 385–405.

Shelman, E.A. & Lazoritz, S. (1999) *Out of the darkness: The story of Mary Ellen Wilson*. Baltimore, MD: Dolphin Moon Publishing.

Sherif, M. (1956) Experiments in group conflict. *Scientific American, 195*, 54–58.

Sieber, J.E. (1992) *Planning Ethically Responsible Research: A Guide for Students and Internal Review Boards*. London: Sage.

Sieber, J.E. & Stanley, B. (1988) Ethical and professional dimensions of socially sensitive research. *American Psychologist, 43*, 49–55.

Singer, P. (1975) *Animal Liberation*. New York: Avon.

Singer, P. (1991) Speciesism, morality and biology: A response to Jeffrey Gray. *The Psychologist, 14*, 199–200.

Singer, P. (2003) Animal liberation at 30. *The New York Review of Books, 50*(8).

Skinner, B.F. (1960) Pigeons in a pelican. *American Psychologist, 15*, 28–37.

Slater, L. (2004) *Opening Skinner's Box: Great Psychological Experiments of the Twentieth Century.* New York: W.W. Norton.

Sloboda, J. (2001, November 22) *Psychologists and Public Policy: Ethical Dilemmas.* Paper presented at the European School of Psychologists for Research, Information and Exchange (ESPRIE), London.

Sloboda, J. & Coleman, P. (2001) Taking a stand. *The Psychologist, 13*(11), 550–551.

Smith, S. & Lewty, W. (1959) Perceptual isolation using a silent room. *Lancet,12*, 342–345.

Smith, P.B. & Bond, M.H. (1993) *Social Psychology Across Cultures.* Hemel Hempstead: Harvester Wheatsheaf.

Sneddon, L.U., Braithwaite, V.A., Gentle, M.J., Broughton, B. & Knight, P. (2003) Trout trauma puts anglers on the hook. *Proceedings from the Royal Society: Biological Sciences, 270* (no.1520).

Solberg, L.C., Baum, A.E., Ahmadiyeh, N., Shimomura, K., Li, R., Turek, F.W., Takahashi, J.S., Churchill, G.A. & Redei, E.E. (2006) Genetic analysis of the stress-responsive adrenocortical axis. *Physiological Genomics, 27*, 362–369.

Soldz, S. (2007) A profession struggles to save its soul: Psychologists, Guantanamo and torture. *Psychoanalytic Activist.* Washington, DC: American Psychological Association.

Stein, M.B., Walker, J.R. & Forde, D.R. (1996) Public-speaking fears in a community sample: Prevalence, impact on functioning and diagnostic classification. *Archives of General Psychiatry, 53*(2).

Stevens, M.J. & Gielen, U.P. (Eds.) (2007) *Toward a Global Psychology: Theory, Research, Intervention, and Pedagogy.* Mahwah, NJ: Lawrence Erlbaum Associates.

Summerfield, D. (2000) War and mental health: A brief overview. *British Medical Journal, 321*, 232–235.

Tajfel, H. (1970) Experiments in intergroup discrimination. *Scientific American, 223*, 96–102.

The Guardian (2003, January 29) Kick 'em while they're down. Retrieved July 11, 2003. from http://media.guardian.co.uk/broadcast/comment/0,7493,996086,00.html

Treaty of Lisbon (2009) Retrieved February 2011 from http://eurlex.europa.eu/JOHtml_do?uri=OJ:C:2007:306:SOM:EN:HTML

Triunfol, M.L. (2003) Barebacking and bag chasers: expressions of an HIV subculture. *AIDScience, 3*, http://aidscience.org/Articles/aidscience030.asp

Tunnicliff, P.L. (1998) Ethics of Experimentation: A Replication without Deception. Retrieved July 2005 from http://www.faculty.sfasu.edu/gford/EthicsofExperimentation.htm

Understanding Animal Research (2010) *BUAV Student Guide: Economical with the Truth.* Retrieved June 2010 from http://www.understanding animalresearch.org.uk/latest_news/blog/show/184/buav_student_guide_ economical_with_the_truth

United Nations' Universal Declaration of Human Rights (1948) Retrieved February 11, 2011, from http://www.un.org/en/documents/udhr/index.shtml

Van Gelder, L. (1985) The strange case of the electronic lover. *Ms, 117,* 123– 124.

Weisstein, N. (1992) Psychology constructs the female, or the fantasy life of the male psychologist (with some attention to the fantasies of his friends the male biologist and the male anthropologist). In J.S. Bohan (Ed.), *Seldom Seen, Rarely Heard: Women's Place in Psychology* (pp. 61–78). Boulder, CO: Westview.

Westin, A.F. (1967) *Privacy and Freedom.* New York: Atheneum.

Whyte, W.F. (1943) *Street Corner Society: Social Structure of an Italian Slum.* Chicago: University of Chicago Press.

Wilson, D. (2005, August 13) *Big Brother* damages our health. *The Guardian.* Retrieved May 2010 from http://www.guardian.co.uk/media/2005/aug/13/ bigbrother.comment

Wilson, D. (2009) *A History of British Serial Killing 1888–2008.* London: Sphere.

Windle, C. & Vallance, T. (1964) The future of military psychology: Paramilitary psychology. *American Psychologist, 19,* 128.

Wiseman, R. (2010) Personal communication. Retrieved February 2010 from http://en.wordpress.com/tag/quirky-stuff/

Zubek, J.P. (1969) *Sensory Deprivation: Fifteen Years of Research.* New York: Appleton-Century-Croft.

Index

Entries in bold denote Key Term with definition.